THE PORT OF Penzance

The lookout onboard the Isles of Scilly steamer Lyonesse *keeping a sharp watch as she approaches the islands in thick fog in the summer of 1900.*

Clive Carter

Penzance harbour in the 1890s by local photographer Preston. Already the rather natty barque, with the white-painted ports, in the coal berth was becoming a rare sight as Penzance relied more upon coastal shipping, especially coal boats, rather than cargoes landed by deep water sailing vessels such as this. Indeed, a small coasting ketch and a steam collier can be seen unloading.

Contents

Little girls at play on the beach, Mount's Bay, 1920s.
Front cover; The Kruzensthern in Mount's Bay, 1996
Rear cover; *Author's painting of the loss of the* Mary James, *1901.*

Designed by Neil Parkhouse

British Library Cataloguing-in-Publication Data. A catalogue record for this book is available from the British Library.

ISBN 0 9533028 0 6

Black Dwarf Publications
47 – 49 High Street, Lydney, Gloucestershire GL15 5DD

Cover design and page makeup by Artytype, 5 The Marina, Harbour Road, Lydney, Gloucestershire GL15 4ET
Printed by APB Process Print, Bristol

A Message from the Town Mayor

When I was told a book was to be written about Penzance Harbour, I was delighted. Although the subject had been touched upon in P.A.S. Pool's 'History of Penzance', the history of the harbour is one that should have been recorded years ago. Its influence upon Penzance in financial, social and, above all, anecdotal terms, is a story well worth telling and I hope you enjoy it.

Councillor Mrs Caroline White
Town Mayor of Penzance

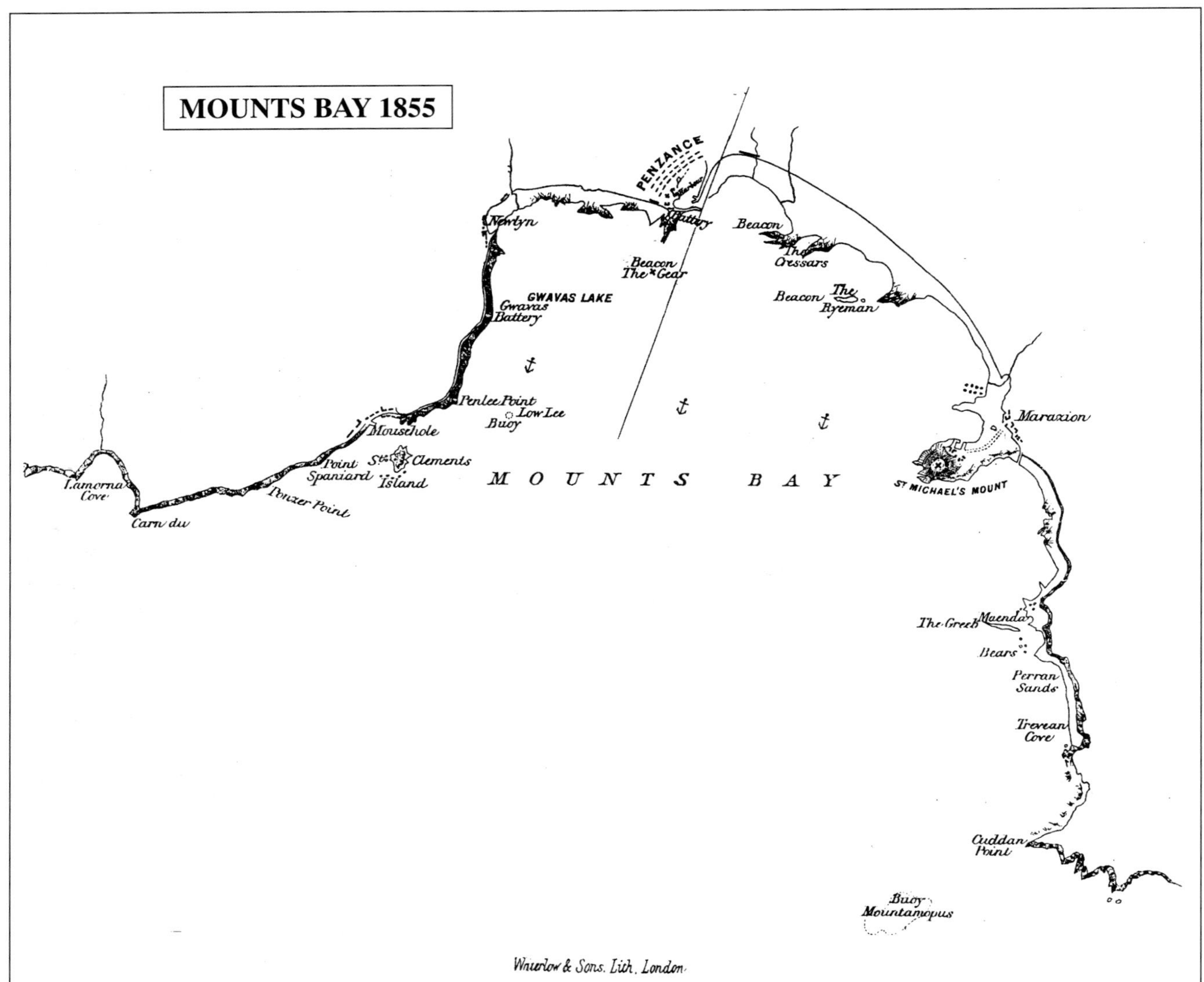

Acknowledgements

The author is indebted to the following people, organisations and civic bodies: The Lady Mayor of Penzance; Penzance Town Council; Penwith District Council; Penlee Branch R.N.L.I.; J.H. Bennetts Ltd.; Isles of Scilly Steamship Co.; Corporation of Trinity House; Penzance Library, Morrab Gardens; Trinity House National Lighthouse Centre; Penzance Public Library; The National Trust; Penlee House Museum; Neil Clark, Harbour Master, Penzance; A.F.M. Holman; K. Kestle; John Corin; David Jones; W. Johns; Mike Mellows; R.B. Paul; F.E. Gibson; Theo Barrett; Phil Moncton; Captain Steve Palk; Captain Alan Riggall; Andrew Hallam; Norman Williams; Gustav Raamsdonk; to Eric Collins, Fred Edwards, 'Duggie' Drew and Walter Tuffle, all sadly no longer with us and lastly, especially to Glyn Richards of Newlyn for permission to use his photographs of classic ships.

Chapter 1

Pirates, Smugglers and Spanish Invaders

'Pensants, about a Myle from Mowsehole, stonding fast in the Shore of Montbay, ys the Westest Market Towne of al Cornwayle, and no Socur for Botes or Shyppes but a forsed Pere or Key.' John Leland, 1538.

The original rough stone pier as it would have appeared in the 14th and 15th centuries, when Penzance was first granted its weekly market.

Jutting far out into the western seaways, Cornwall has a maritime heritage that is inseparable from the Atlantic rim of Europe and to sail into the ancient harbour of Penzance is to follow in the wake of generations of seafarers who navigated the Celtic seas. Lying on the westerly shores of Mount's Bay, this Cornish port was once a medieval fishing 'porth', where ships that berthed alongside the rough stone pier paid dues to the Lords of the Manor of Alverton. The little harbour was sheltered by a rocky headland, crowned by a small chapel dedicated to St. Anthony, which gave the town its name - 'Pensans' or Penzance, literally 'The Holy Headland'.

In 1332, Penzance was busy enough for King Edward I to grant the town a weekly market and also an annual fair during the Festival of St. Peter on the 29th of June. Ships loaded or discharged cargoes of wine, pottery, iron, timber, fish and tin, and for centuries devout Cornish pilgrims also embarked for the great Catholic Shrine of Santiago de Compostella in Spain. In 1424, John Nycholl was granted a licence to voyage to Galicia in the *Katherine* of Penzance, a frail round bowed barque which spent years ferrying pilgrims through the Atlantic gales. The same John Nycholl later commanded the barque *Michael* of Penzance, which in the season of 1434 alone took 200 pilgrims to Santiago.

By the time of Queen Elizabeth I, Penzance Quay was often so crowded that Cornish sailors found themselves lying yardarm to yardarm with ships from all over the known world - 'Urcas' and flyboats from Flanders and Spain, merchantmen from the Baltic known as 'Easterlings', pinnaces manned by Scots, Irishmen or Basques, and English men-o-war with their great castles bristling with cannons. They came to trade, to smuggle or to shelter from storms. Often, too, they came to fight when wars on continental Europe spilled over into the western Atlantic. Then, sailing as pirates, privateers or under a Royal Ensign, they fought with daring and unbelievable savagery for command of the ocean seas.

To protect Penzance, the Queen's father, Henry VIII, built on the headland above the harbour a small fort or 'Barbican', whose name is still preserved 400 years later by one of the most historic buildings on the waterfront and also in the local street name 'Barbican Lane'.

Penzance was also a landfall for the robust Tudor sailors, homeward bound after harrying the Spaniards or exploring the 'New World'; indeed, according to legend, the first tobacco smoked in England was by Sir Walter Raleigh on the pier head here. Queen Elizabeth's admirals also relied upon the guns of

The coast around Penzance has been witness to the destruction of many an unfortunate vessel over the centuries. One of the earliest wrecks recorded was that of a small galleon captured by George Clifford, Earl of Cumberland, on the Spanish Main in the summer of 1589. He sent her home as a 'prize' in the following winter, complete with a fabulous cargo of looted silver and under the command of close friend Captain Christopher Lister, who had been a prisoner of Barbary pirates for a number of years, but, caught by a gale, she was lost with all hands near Penzance.

nearby St. Michael's Mount, a rocky islet crowned by a monastery fortress and which gave the bay its name. In the winter of 1565, John Hawkins arrived in the bay in the *Minion*, after a disastrous voyage when his squadron of vessels was ambushed by a Spanish 'Flota', in the Mexican port of San Juan de Ullao.

The Spaniards themselves struck Penzance on a July morning in 1595, in an action that looms large in the town's history but was only a small part of the long drawn out fight for supremacy in the Atlantic and over the riches to be had from the 'New World' of the Americas. Briefly, Drake and Hawkins were assembling a task force of men and ships in Plymouth, with which to attack Panama. The Spanish raid was by way of being a reconnaissance and also, if enough mayhem could be caused, in the hope of upsetting Drake's plans. A galley squadron landed six hundred pikemen and musketeers in Penzance, having already burned Newlyn and Mousehole, two other small ports in Mount's Bay. The Cornish Militia rallied briefly among the towans, now covered by the modern promenade, but were driven back into the town. Sir Francis Godolphin attempted to make a stand in the Market Place until, most of his men having bolted at the sight of the advancing Spanish infantry, he too was forced to gallop away towards St. Michael's Mount.

The Spanish raid of 1595. Musketeers and pikemen march through the burning streets of Penzance.
'Y a-wra tyra war mldy Merlyn, a-wra gesky Pawl, Pensans ha Newlyn.'
'They shall land on the rock of Merlyn, who shall burn Paul, Penzance and Newlyn.'

The raiders marched down historic Chapel Street, or 'Our Lady Street' as it was then known, admiring the handsome houses before setting them ablaze. Ships in the harbour were also burned but the ancient Chapel of St. Mary's was spared through the intercession of 'Ricardo Bourley', alias Richard Burley, an English Catholic in the service of King Phillip of Spain. Although Burley had organised the raid, he stayed the firebrands by recalling how mass had been said in the chapel during the days of Queen Mary. This remarkable occasion was commemorated by the squadron's chaplain, Friar Domingo Martinez, who rapidly composed two verses in English explaining why St. Mary's was spared and expressed his faith in God that mass would be said again in the chapel within two years; all was duly written on parchment and nailed to the main door.

The Spaniards held Penzance for the next two days, during which they celebrated a mass on the open beach on the eve of St. James's Day. They even sent a boat ashore and carried off a bronze cannon from the Barbican battery, as good English ordinance was always highly valued back in Spain. On the third morning, the galley squadron rowed close to St. Michael's Mount but the Cornish forces had rallied on the sands and kept up a heavy fire on the raiders. By then the wind had veered north west and, fearing that they might be trapped in Mount's Bay by the English frigates from Plymouth, the Spaniards sailed for their base near

Spanish soldiers looting a highly prized bronze English cannon from the Barbican battery at Penzance during the raid of 1595.

Smugglers bringing in a load of contraband whilst a Customs cutter attempts to head them off.

Lorient, in Brittany.

The bronze cannon which today stands proudly outside the Public Library at Penzance had nothing to do with the Great Armada of 1588, though it does come from a Spanish galleon. Homeward bound from the Indies in February 1635, she was captured and looted by Dutch warships. She put in '*to Guavers Lake . . . . and riding there was cast away*'; she was wrecked on Low Lee Ledge, off Penlee Point. The authorities tried to salvage goods and gear but they were '*opposed by a riotous multitude*', being the inhabitants of Mousehole and Market Jew, who maintained their riot with the cry '*One and all*' – perhaps the first time the now traditional Cornish motto was ever heard.

Two hundred hides were piled on the decks ready to be saved but '*the rebels of Mousehole came in their boats in the night and carried them all away to their homes*'. The Queen's officers who tried to claim them were faced by '*at least 100 men, women and children who came about them with weapons, and not only threatened to kill them, but had done so, if not to save their lives they had not all three leapt down a steep cliff*'.

The cannon was raised by the salvage ship *Greencastle* in 1916. From which vessel this cannon actually came has been the subject of much speculation over the years and the author only discovered the description of the wreck as this book was in final preparation; unfortunately, it did not include the galleon's name.

The infamous Spanish raid of 1595 left both town and harbour in ruins but Penzance recovered and was soon granted a new Royal Charter. Yet there were further turbulent times ahead as the Cornish chose to fight for King Charles I during the English Civil War. Already Penzance was just one of the many Cornish ports from where wool and tin ingots were being smuggled onboard ships bound for Flanders; the money raised from the sale of these illicit cargoes bought muskets, pikes, powder and shot to arm the Cornish troops.

Across the bay, St. Michael's Mount was held for the King by the old Royalist knight Sir Francis Basset, who spent a fortune building extra fortifications and maintaining a garrison of gunners and musketeers. Unfortunately, to no avail as, harrassed by the Roundhead army and Parliamentry frigates, the Mount finally surrendered in April 1646. Penzance remained loyal to the King and consequently was rewarded with being sacked by the Parliamentary general Sir Thomas Fairfax.

Trade by sea increased and the first harbour was built in the 1760s, the new quays being kept busy during the long wars against the French. The bay was often filled by convoys of British merchantmen, homeward bound from the Indies, Bengal or the Carolinas. In November 1779, a Newlyn fisherman recorded; '*Came into Gwavas lake his Majesty's sloop,* 'the squirl'*, with abt. 52 vessels more under convoy bound for North channels*'. The Royal Navy often had to fight off heavily gunned privateers from Brest or St. Malo but was far less welcome when they sent press gangs into the narrow streets around the town.

The French cannon, raised from the wreck of a Spanish galleon by the *Greencastle* in 1916, outside the Public Library.

Penzance retains a unique place in naval history as, in October 1805, the schooner of war *Pickle*, homeward bound after the Battle of Trafalgar, spoke the news of Lord Nelson's death to some of the port's fishing boats. They hurriedly sailed home and the sad tidings were announced from the gallery of the historic 'Union Hotel' in Chapel Street. A procession, headed by the Mayor and a large banner bearing the legend *'Mourn for the Brave, the Glorious Nelson gone, His Last Sea Fight is Fought, His Work of Glory Done'*, marched up to the Madron Church, a custom that is still honoured each year on the anniversary of Trafalgar by the presence of the Royal Navy.

The Royal Navy and the Customs men had also to contend with the Cornish smugglers, especially the Carter brothers, John and Henry. John Carter, because of his daring and defiance of the English crown, was known as the 'King of Prussia', while the rocky inlet where he kept his smuggling cutter was called 'Prussia Cove'. He remained a sober and 'honest' businessman, keeping his customers happy with regular cargoes of brandy, wines and luxuries from Morlaix and Roscoff. Indeed, John Carter was so honest that, after the customs seized some of his contraband, he broke into the bonded stores at Penzance but made sure that he only took back the goods that belonged to him!

The brig *Fairy* at the quay wall in front of the Dolphin Inn, in the early 19th century.

Today, all that remains of this rumbustious era is John Carter's autobiography, written after he had relinquished smuggling for religion, while Prussia Cove is a small fishing inlet much visited by tourists.

Prussia Cove on a 1920s postcard. The era of the Carter brothers was long gone and it was by this time just a peaceful tourist spot.

Despite the smuggling and sea battles in Mount's Bay, Penzance became one of the busiest ports in Cornwall. Right in front of the Dolphin Inn, now over three hundred years old, was the 'Tin Man's Haul', a tiny cove where three small brigs, the *Fairy*, the *Basset* and the *Prince of Wales*, refitted between voyages to London with ingot tin. The landlord of the Dolphin, William Treluddra, also accepted parcels and goods for the Isles of Scilly, sent on board the brig *Lord Howe* or the cutter *Ariadne*. His thriving business was often interrupted by hard easterly gales, when waves broke over the Dolphin leaving bottles and barrels bobbing about in the flooded cellar!

The Dolphin was also the meeting place for wealthy town merchants like Sir Rose Price, who made such a fortune in the Jamaican rum trade that, on returning home, he bought Trengwainton Manor. He lived extravagantly but died bankrupt in 1834, leaving behind a row of cottages named Jamaica Terrace and a large granite mausoleum in Madron church yard. Richard Oxnam, who lived at 'The Abbey', also made and lost a fortune, though he speculated in Cornish mining. Another town merchant in the rum trade was Lemon Hart, a member of Penzance's large Jewish community, who supplied 'grog' to Nelson's Navy from his cellars in Quay Street.

William Davies Mathews, a Welsh sea captain and ship owner who had settled in Penzance, built the port's original dry dock, which docked its first vessel, the *Mary* of Hamburg, in January 1815. Many tales were told of this dry dock, the gates of which opened straight into the harbour. A sail maker was almost skewered once, when a small clipper fell over in the dock and her topsail yardarm came through the roof of his hut.

On another remarkable occasion a tidal wave created by a submarine earthquake, far out in the Atlantic, carried away the dry dock gates and threatened to capsize the brig *Lord Howe*, which was fitting out for a voyage to the West Indies. The yard apprentices dragged a hawser up Dock Lane to Admiral Lindsay's house, and one lad climbed the coach house wall and opened the garden gate. The hawser was quickly secured to an elm tree, holding the brig safely as more waves rushed into the dry dock. The old Admiral, roused by the noise and unaware of the danger, threatened to cut the hawser but a young apprentice dared him to try it. Next day, the Admiral called at the dry dock and presented the lad with five shillings, saying 'Always do your duty young man.'

Chapter 2
The Victorian Harbour

'SEPT. 6 1868. 6 A.M. went into harbour and moored alongside the East Quay, which like the West Quay . . . is encumbered with filth and coal-dust, that nothing short of real distress will drive me into the nasty harbour again.' R.T. McMullen, 'Down Channel', 1891.

An engraving of St. Michael's Mount at the time of the visit of Prince Albert and Queen Victoria to Penzance in 1845. The Royal Yacht can be seen on the right and the bay is crowded with small craft that have come out to greet it. As often with Victorian art, the Mount has been somewhat 'dramatised' by being made to appear both higher and steeper than it actually was.

By 1845, Penzance harbour was sheltered from southerly gales by the long Albert Pier, named in his own honour by the Prince Consort when he and Queen Victoria visited Mount's Bay in the Royal Yacht. The south pier was extended to its modern length in 1853 and crowned by the, now familiar, graceful white lighthouse, built from rings of iron cast by the famous Copperhouse Foundry in Hayle. Today the Albert Pier is home to the Yacht Club, the Diving Club and a small engineering works.

Penzance matured as a bustling Victorian seaport and market town, as new streets climbed the hills above it and elegant villas dotted the outskirts. The mild climate attracted visitors, bathing machines stood alongside the luggers, seine boats beached off the promenade, and hotels and guest houses, many of them kept by the wives or spinster daughters of sea captains, overlooked the bay.

For nearly a century, Penzance also had a large 'blue water fleet', manned by the pick of Mount's Bay sailors and captains. Their voyaging in deep water made the yellow hills of Morocco or Gallipoli as familiar as their own Cornish moors. Mates and masters could navigate through the Greek Islands or Mexican Isthmus as easily as threading the shoals of Scilly or Mount's Bay. One Penzance sailor became bosun of the legendary clipper *Cutty Sark* and another Bay mariner served as purser of a Confederate blockade runner during the American Civil War, until a Union gunboat sank her off the Delaware. One Penzance brigantine, the *Arethusa*, commanded by a staunch Wesleyan, Captain Richard Quance, was on her annual voyage to fetch hides from Rio Grande du Sul when she was rammed by a whale off the Brazilian coast. Another local brigantine, the *Propontis*, took the first Christian missionary to Burma and voyaged as far as Vietnam. Captain Johnson of Penzance commanded the schooner *Devil* which, complete with satanic figurehead, was so fast she overtook a Cunard steam tug in Queenstown Roads.

There was the oddly named schooner *Ready Rhino*, colloquial Cornish for 'ready cash', which was commanded by Captain William Strike and manned by his family from Porthleven. She sailed deepwater for decades and, in September

A turn of the century postcard view of St. Michael's Mount – compare it with the artist's impression above. The rowing boats are ferries, to take tourists to the Mount when the tide was in.

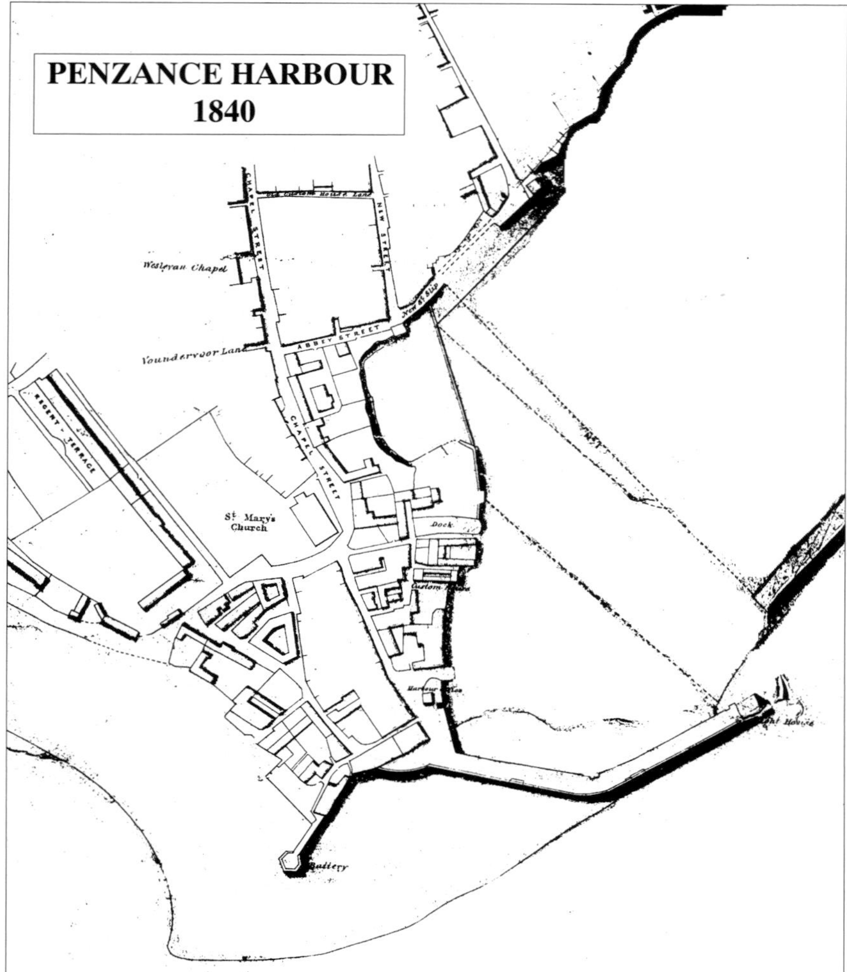

Note the dry dock with its west facing entrance and that the tide could reach around the Custom House and Trinity Yard, now separated from the quay by Madron Road. The map showed proposed improvements to the harbour; note the line of the quay at the top and the pier, right. The Albert Pier, completed in 1845, was built on a different alignment to that shown here – see 1865 map.

Victorian Penzance in all its glory! This is Market Jew Street around 1895; the prosperity that the harbour and the railway brought to the town is evident. The name, incidentally, is derived from the Cornish *Marghas Yow* – literally Market Thursday, the day when the market was held in the street.

1866, was the first British vessel to enter the port of Boca, '*having on board two locomotives for the Western Railway . . . . we have no doubt those friends of Buenos Aires who may meet him on the Liverpool Exchange will warmly congratulate him on his success in landing the locomotives without the troublesome intervention of lighters.*'

Many Penzance sailors had shivered with 'yellow jack' fever in their bunks at Pelatus or Rio Grande; dozens more, '*rigged in a suit of canvas with the last stitch through the nose*', had been buried over the side everywhere from Palermo to Cox's Bazaar. When Captain George Gruzelier, of Mousehole, died at Mobile, Alabama in April 1870, his brother, the Chief Officer, brought the ship home but it was noted that his other brother Richard Gruzelier had already 'died foreign', as indeed had a dozen other masters from that one small village in Mount's Bay.

Since the 1840s, Penzance had been a regular port of call for many of the small coastwise packets, which often 'called off', as it was termed, sending in their boats to transfer cargo or passengers rather than risk coming alongside the exposed quay. The newspaper cutting below, detailing the sailings of the packets *Pioneer* and *Clifton* on a regular London–Bristol run in 1857, calling at Penzance and Falmouth, is an example of the type of service offered. The *Pioneer* was herself wrecked inward bound to Penzance in February 1865, when she foundered on the Runnelstone whilst rounding Land's End under steam and sail.

STEAM COMMUNICATION BETWEEN
BRISTOL AND LONDON,
Calling at PENZANCE and FALMOUTH, (wind and weather permitting,) with or without Pilots, and liberty to tow vessels.
THE FIRST CLASS SCREW STEAMSHIPS
"PIONEER" and "CLIFTON,"
are intended to sail with Goods and Passengers during month of JUNE, 1857, as under: —
Bristol to Penzance, and thence to Falmouth and London
Wednesday, June 3rd
" " 17th

It was from the 1840s also, that Penzance's other role, as a tourist resort, began to grow in importance, concurrent with the calling of the packets. However, this new source of income had to be provided for, which led, in 1843, to the start of construction of the celebrated promenade, a feature which remains popular with townspeople and tourists alike to this day. Twice it has been demolished by south-easterly gales and the long sandy beach, where luggers once 'payed up' to dry out and mend their nets, has now vanished, leaving only 'bullies', the local name for shingle rock. One of the worst storms occurred in October 1880, when Mount's Bay was swept by a hurricane coming in from the south south east. The huge seas engendered swallowed the lugger *Jane* just seaward of Penzance pierhead and badly damaged the new harbour works as well as partly demolishing the promenade.

Many small Penzance ships sailed to New York with Cornish emmigrants, mostly Cousin

A less commonly seen view of Penzance is from the hills above Newlyn. This 1895 photograph shows the westerly extent of the town, prior to the development of the area known as Lodga, where the seine boats payed up, and the sea front right round to Newlyn. The harbour can be glimpsed in the right distance and prominent in the centre are Bodilly's steam flour mills. Note also the size and quality of the housing on view – those who had made their money seafaring, ship owning and merchanting had spent it wisely. The unknown photographer has aroused a little bovine curiosity.

The promenade beach in the late 1870s, showing a number of Penzance luggers 'payed up', whilst their nets are dried and mended. The yards and yards of black netting are laid out on the sand that covered this beach then, all washed away by storms by the end of the 19th century, leaving the shingle which is all that remains to this day.

Sailing trawlers and town schooners crowd the mud off the South Quay, which, until the building of the wet dock in the 1880s, provided uncertain shelter from the vagueries of the weather. Ships moored up to the big iron harbour buoys or just to quay posts but it was no guarantee against being swept away, as happened with the brigantine *Hero*, of Bideford.

The State Barge belonging to St. Michael's Mount was already ancient when photographed in the Mount harbour about 1875.

A dramatic photograph of the promenade after the great storm of 1880, showing the sea still boiling against the battered frontage. The man in the foreground is Fred Rodda (with his young son), well known printer in the town. Morrab Road commenced to be made in 1881 and the Royal Baths on the esplanade, behind the furthest figure, were taken down in 1883. The view below, looking the opposite way towards the harbour, was probably taken in the spring of 1881 and shows the rebuilding of the promenade in hand, following the storm of the previous October. A local lugger lands granite blocks to repair the wall and, as well as the period costumes, note the magnificent example of a Victorian push chair in the foreground.

EMIGRATION TO AMERICA.

DIRECT

FROM PENZANCE TO NEW YORK.

The Fine A.E. 1, Coppered Fast-Sailing Ship

"OREGON,"

THREE HUNDRED TONS BURTHEN,

ROULLE CARY, *Commander*,

WILL, weather permitting, sail from Penzance on the FIRST of APRIL.

The *Oregon* has very superior accommodations for both Cabin and Steerage Passengers, and every precaution will be taken to promote their health and comfort. Provisions will be found them at the Ship's expense, until the arrival of the vessel at New York.

The Captain is well experienced in the trade, and this affords an excellent opportunity for Passengers to any part of the UNITED STATES.

The Owner will give Letters to Farmers and Mechanics to Parties in Michigan and Utica, who can put them in the way of procuring employment; and to those desirous of settling on Lands, how to manage for Farms to the best advantage.

To Miners also, this affords a favourable opportunity, and the Owner being acquainted with some of the Proprietors of Mines, Letters of recommendation will be given to Passengers who can produce satisfactory testimonials of character, &c.

As the *Oregon* will take only a limited number of Passengers, an early application should be made to the Owner, at *Treneere;* W. C. Hemmings, *Penzance;* Wm. Brown, *St. Austell;* Thomas Corfield, *Penryn;* G. J. Phillips, *Camborne;* & at the Office, *Roseworthy*.

Dated 9th February, 1852.

Jacks and Aunt Jennies bound for the mining fields of California or the Great Lakes. In the spring of 1854, the *Oregon*, the vessel mentioned in the cutting above, was steering a southerly course to avoid icebergs when a northerly hurricane drove her down to the Azores. Three of the one hundred passengers on board were too frightened even to go below and so spent the storm lashed to the mizzen mast. Despite this, the vessel made a safe arrival in New York, where the grateful passengers presented the master, Captain Chivers, with a testimonial and a purse of gold.

Following a visit by the eminent engineer Isambard Kingdom Brunel in 1850, to survey the route to the town from Hayle on behalf of the West Cornwall Railway, the '*first locomotive that ever skirted the shores of Mount's Bay*' arrived at Penzance station, a commodious structure of wood, on 25 February 1852, the official opening taking place six months later with the completion of the line through to Truro. The coming of the railway drastically altered the bay shoreline towards Penzance, especially the building of a long wooden viaduct leading into the terminus which, despite being washed away by storms several times, was not finally replaced until the 1930s.

From 1859, with the opening of Brunel's Royal Albert Bridge across the Tamar at Saltash, Penzance was at last connected to London, although the break of gauge at Truro – the GWR line was broad gauge and the West Cornwall standard – meant all traffic had to be transshipped there. The linking of Penzance with the capital's markets brought enormous benefits for the farmers, market gardeners and fishermen of the locality, especially once the broad gauge line of the Great Western Railway finally arrived late in 1866 meaning that, at last, services could work straight through. Luggers raced each other to get their catch on the night expresses or 'fish specials' that ensured Cornish mackerel, packed in locally made ice, reached Billingsgate just twelve hours after they had been swimming around the Wolf Rock. In later years, cured fish was shipped from Penzance to Italy by fast steamers, which also took ingot tin from Chyandour and Treriefe smelters, and their success drove the old-time Cornish fish schooner from the Mediterranean.

By 1884, the harbour had been rebuilt and extended by the construction of Wharf Road, from the railway station to what is still today the modern floating dock. This new waterfront buried

GWR No. 3418 *Paddington* brings an express into Penzance across the wooden viaduct in the summer of 1904.

The schooner *Mary James* photographed leaving Penzance in 1901, shortly before she was lost near the Longships.

the old foreshore, including a tiny drydock and grid iron, and the old public baths, which for years had been used by a shipwright. The 'Tin Mans' Haul' also disappeared, though the name would be used for another generation at least.

SCHOONER FOR SALE.

TO BE SOLD, by auction (unless previously disposed of by private contract) on Thursday, the 26th day of May inst., at 4 o'clock in the afternoon, at the AUCTION ROOMS, 54 and 55, Causewayhead, Penzance, all that

EXCELLENT SCHOONER, THE *MARY JAMES*, of Penzance, as she now lies in the harbour, with her boats, stores, and appurtenances.

Was built at Padstow in 1862, classed eight years A. 1., register 163 tons, carries 280 tons, and draws 12½ feet.

May be viewed on application to the shipkeeper, on board; and other particulars of

W. HOSKEN RICHARDS,
Auctioneer, &c., Penzance.

Dated, 10th May, 1870.

Many town schooners were owned by the mining families at St. Just and spent their careers hauling copper ore to Wales, returning with coal for the mine engines. Often they were delayed by gales and would be met by long convoys of waggons driven by tough and reckless waggoners, dressed in 'Billycock hats and Sandford frocks', who used fists, whips and wheel hubs to be first into a berth. Once loaded, they raced throughout the narrow streets, showering coal over the townspeople, often wrecking market stalls or shopfront windows.

The story of the schooner *Mary James* provides a typical example of the life and times of such vessels. She was built in 1862 by Richard Tredwen of Padstow and was forever known as 'The Sabbath Breaker' because, having stuck on her launching, she came free of her own accord the following Sunday. She was owned for most of her life by the mining family of Harvey James of St. Just, after whose wife she was named. She made endless voyages hauling copper ore from the St. Just mines to Wales and returning with coal for the mine engines. She also went foreign and was renowned as a fast vessel; in 1870 she ran from Greenock to Penzance in 60 hours under Captain Legg of Scilly, who later commanded the Liverpool clipper *Cairnsmore*.

The *Mary James* had her narrow escapes too. She survived being blown ashore on Mumbles beach and once, having parted warps outside Penzance harbour, drifted stern first almost onto the Cressars Rocks. Those

Two photographs of the harbour reconstruction during the early 1880s. The view **top** shows a steam crane busy laying the new granite dock wall which, by early 1882, was already masking the old South Quay. The new quays were created by back filling with mine dirt from old Wheal Bolton, near Ludguan, though the carters were not above dumping rubbish and ballast. Indeed, one part of the quay actually collapsed after strong tides scoured out the filling. The photograph **lower** is looking along the line of South Quay, across the bay, with the wooden railway viaduct just visible in the background. The wooden staging marks the position of where the entrance to the wet dock was to be.

An unusual view of the harbour taken in the late 1890s, showing it packed as the Lowestoft sailing trawler fleet shelters from a heavy storm.

on board were rescued by the lifeboat and the *Mary James* herself was winched clear by the Trinity steamer *Alert*. 'Neptune's Junkyard' finally claimed her on a stormy November morning in 1901, when she was dismasted off Longships. The Penzance coaster *India* and a Sennen gig tried and failed to get a tow line on board. Reluctantly, Captain Warren and his crew abandoned the stricken schooner for the Sennen lifeboat. At dawn, wreckage washing about the Brissons Rocks was all that was left to mark the end of the old schooner, only a few miles from where her owners once lived.

Frequent callers were the small Norwegian brigs which landed timber for the tin mines, though they only came during the summer months when the Baltic was free of ice. Their tall fair-haired crews were popular both at Penzance and across the bay at St. Michael's Mount, though the latter harbour was more open to gales and masters needed to take extra care. Indeed, in November 1865 the brig *Rhederenden* of Porsgrund was washed out of the pier and wrecked on the beach.

Until the building of the wet dock in the 1880s, many vessels used to berth on the mud off the South Quay, although it provided very uncertain shelter. Ships were moored up to the big iron harbour buoys positioned there or, if none were free, tied to wooden quay posts but there was always the risk of being swept away from these exposed positions in inclement weather. In February 1861, the Bideford polacca brigantine *Hero* was plucked from its moorings along the South Quay in a SSW hurricane and, in a brave but foolhardy attempt to save her, four of her own crew and two other schoonermen were drowned.

Penzance, being a busy commercial port, never had a fishery to rival Newlyn, though one of the largest Mount's Bay luggers, the *Children's Friend*, was launched in June 1898 by Joe Legg; his shipwright's shop and small slipway has long lain buried under the dry dock's blacksmith's shop, in the corner of the Abbey Basin. Most fishing boats came in just to land their catches, refit or just to shelter, as on a stormy winters day in 1890. It is perhaps significant that during the Newlyn Riots of 1896, the Penzance men joined up with the Lowestoft men in the latter's violent dispute over Sunday fishing with the Newlyn fishermen.

The 1880s improvements were the zenith of development at Penzance harbour. The end of the nineteenth century saw the changeover from sail to steam gathering greater pace, although it was to be another fifty years before sailing coasters finally ceased to call. The compact wet dock, the new dry dock and the vast expanse of harbour enclosed behind the Albert Pier, were to prove of sufficient capacity to meet the needs of cargo and shipping at Penzance right up until the contractions of the 1950s.

In the 19th century the harbour was often crowded with sailing craft. Centre foreground, moored at the West Quay, is the schooner *Crapa* of Stavanger, one of the many Norwegian vessels that brought timber for the mines. Beyond, a veritable forest of masts rises from the assortment of coastwise sail alongside the Albert Pier.

A photograph showing the new wet dock, crowded with shipping in the 1890s. In the foreground is a large wood capstan, used to warp vessels through the gaps.

A glimpse of the wet dock in the 1890s. A three-masted barquentine sits at the quay and on the left is the granite stone Harbour Office, complete with weighbridge and ornate gas lamp in front. Note the shutters for the windows.

Sailors, children and old timers idle away the day near the battery, on a hot summer's afternoon around 1870 – a pleasant occupation still practised around the harbour today, as is the urge to paint initials or ship names on the quay walls and fences.

The Victorians sense of space and style, when it came to laying out urban landscapes, puts the haphazard and often jarring development of today to shame. This is the view east along the Promenade, or the Esplanade as it was sometimes called, towards the town and harbour in 1895. Construction of this section began in 1843 and it remains one of the most popular parts of Penzance to this day, with tourists and townspeople alike. The small round building on the extreme left was a post office and next to it is the Serpentine Works, where ornamental items and giftware for the tourists was made. By the time of this view, the luggers no longer 'payed up' on the beach to the right.

Although it has never been a fishing port, leaving that honour to Newlyn, all local fishing boats are registered at Penzance with the initials PZ. This includes boats operating from Newlyn, Mousehole, Porthguarra and all other small ports and coves from the Lizard round to – but not including – St. Ives. This 1895 view shows the fleet putting to sea. Principal fish caught were pilchards and mackerel, although the former had been fished out by the end of the 19th century. The arrival of the railway was instrumental in the further development of the industry; fish caught off Land's End could be on sale in the London markets less than 12 hours later.

The station at Penzance, first opened to passengers in 1852. From 1859, the standard gauge line of the West Cornwall Railway connected with the broad gauge of the Cornwall Railway at Truro and thus,via the Bristol & Exeter and the Great Western Railway, to London. This view, taken about 1882, shows the mixed broad and standard gauge track which existed here between 1866, following the takeover of the WCR by the GWR, and the final gauge conversion of 1892. The station and roof were rebuilt by the GWR in 1878-80 and still survive today. The wooden goods sheds are on the left, with some broad gauge wagons in the sidings, and Albert Pier sweeps round beyond. A siding ran through the goods shed and out along the pier. Penzance generated much traffic in fish, vegetables and flowers, as well as goods and mails to and from the the rest of the Penwith peninsula and the Scilly Isles. The GWR had to make do on this cramped site until they were finally given permission to reclaim land on the left and drastically extend the station in 1937.

PENZANCE HARBOUR 1865

A map of the harbour in 1865, at the time the Borough of Penzance purchased the foreshore from the Duchy of Cornwall. Note the alignment of the Albert Pier, as built, compared with that proposed, as on the earlier map.

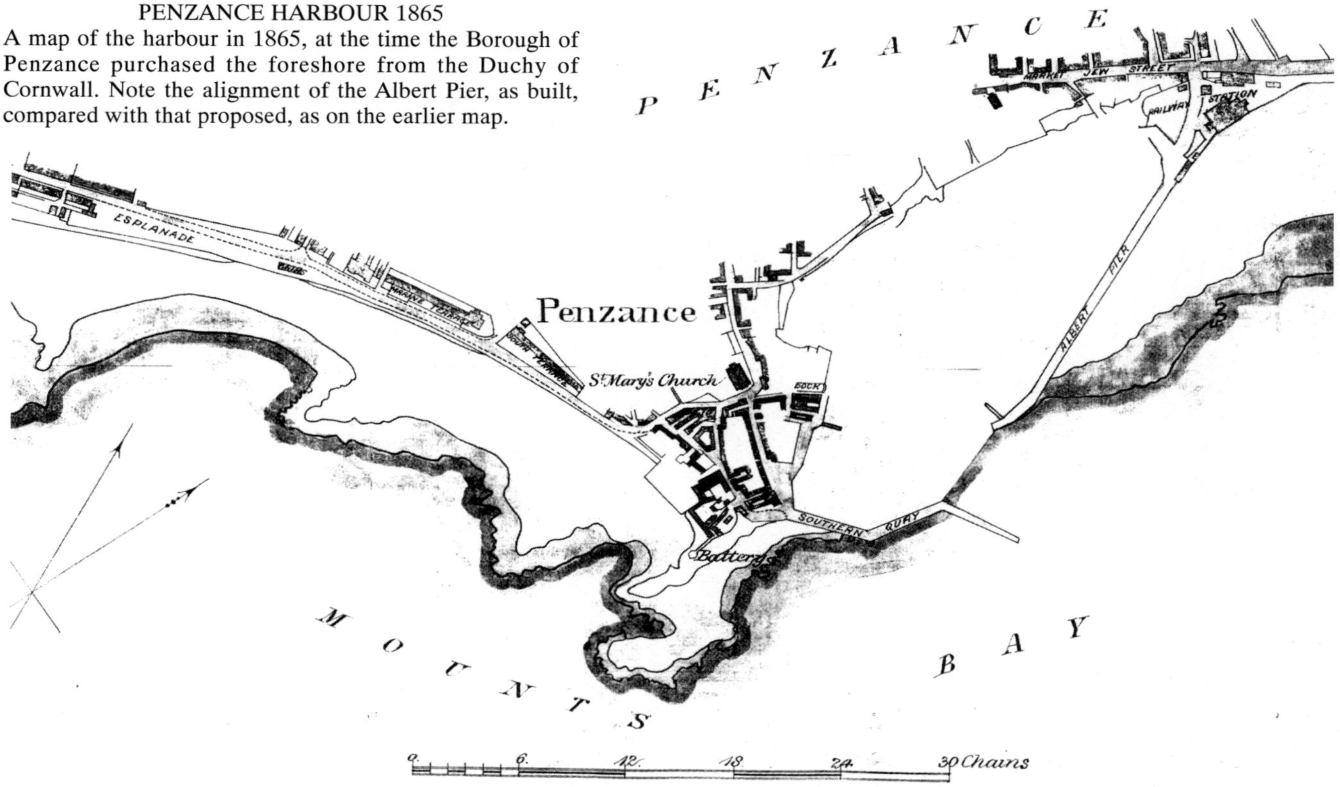

The crowded South Quay and beach in the 1870s, looking towards the Harbour Office, far left. Coal carts are being loaded from the leftmost schooner by means of a boom and wicker baskets. The fully rigged schooner in the centre is most likely taking advantage of a light breeze to dry her sails. In the background, St. Mary's church presides over the scene.

General view over the railway station, harbour and town circa 1885.

Steam from Penzance to Jersey, Guernsey, Liverpool, London, &c.

THE BRISTOL and IRISH STEAM PACKET COMPANY will despatch the STEAM SHIP

CITY OF LIMERICK,

W. BISHOP, Master.

From Liverpool on Sunday, 23rd of April at 7 a.m. **for Jersey and Guernsey, calling at** Penzance, Falmouth, and Plymouth **for Passengers** only, and returning **by same route, leaving Jersey,** Friday, 28th April, 7 a.m., and Guernsey, 11a. m.

FARES to or from PENZANCE.

First Cabin.	Second Cabin.	Deck.
20s.	15s.	10s.

The Screw Steam Ships "Lady Eglinton," and "Nile" or other suitable vessels will leave Penzance for London and Liverpool as under, wind and weather permitting.

FARES.

For London, calling at Falmouth, Plymouth, and Portsmouth	Mon. night,	20s. 15s. 10s.
For Liverpool direct	Tues. night,	15s. 10s. 7s. 6d.

For further information, apply to

W. D. MATHEWS,
Dock Office, Penzance.

A great blizzard struck West Cornwall on 10 March 1891. Due to its southerly latitude, snow is not common in Cornwall and even when it does fall, it rarely settles as thickly as this Christmas card scene, **left**, taken the morning after the blizzard. Among the vessels to be seen in the outer harbour is the Newcastle schooner *James Nicholson*, brought in by the lifeboat at the height of the storm, during which, **right**, the harbour gates collapsed in the teeth of the hurricane accompanying the snow.

A lovely study of St. Michael's Mount taken in 1895 from above Marazion, showing it in all its glory along with the tiny harbour which, over fifty years later, was to be taken over by the salvagors breaking down the wreck of the *Warspite*. Marazion and, in particular, the Mount – in itself, one of the most enduring images of Cornwall – remain popular with visitors today.

Chapter 3
By Sea to Scilly

'. . . the Cherub, *William Tregarthen, master . . . This packet has lately been fitted up with very superior accommodation for ladies and gentlemen, and . . . is better calculated for the comfort of the Passengers than any that has yet sailed to and from the Isles of Scilly.'* Advertisment, Royal Cornwall Gazette, November 1825.

A dramatic photograph of the Scilly Isles packet *Lady of the Isles*, fighting her way into Penzance harbour through heavy seas during a storm in December 1896. For those on board, particularly any passengers, conditions like this must have been terrifying.

Sail soon gave way to steam on the stormy packet run between Penzance and the Isles of Scilly and, by the 1850s, the islands had developed a thriving export trade in fish, flowers and early potatoes, which demanded more than the uncertain sailing of a few tiny schooners. Coming into the islands was 'shopkeepers cargo', farm animals and already the first tourists; there were also ordinary passengers, those who lived on the islands or who had dealings with them wishing to make the trip either way and, most importantly, mail. All of this traffic was soon being accommodated aboard a succession of sturdy iron screw or paddler packet steamers.

The clean and graceful lines of the *Queen of the Bay*, the last of the paddlers to sail on the Scilly service, are shown to good effect as she poses in Penzance harbour around 1885.

The first steamers to visit the Scillies had been excursion packets, in the early 1830s, such as the *Herald* which ran trips from Bristol and Hayle as well as Penzance. From 1842, the *Brilliant* was another regular summer visitor but the economy of the islands was somewhat in the doldrums around this time and consequently pleas by the islanders for their own packet service fell on deaf ears. The improvement in fortunes through the 1850s led, in 1858, to the formation of the Scilly Isles Steam Navigation Company and, at last, a regular steam packet run to the islands commenced.

The *Scotia*, an iron paddler built at Blackwall, was the first on the run, hired as a stopgap from the Chester & Holyhead Railway until the vessel being built for the company, the iron, screw, twin-masted schooner *Little Western*, was ready. She performed sterling service for over a decade before demand, particularly from the mainland, for another service led to the

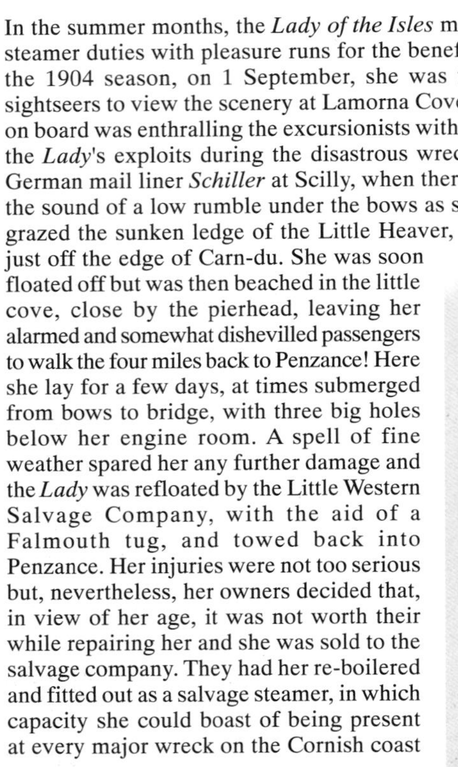

A *Lady* in distress!

In the summer months, the *Lady of the Isles* mixed her regular packet steamer duties with pleasure runs for the benefit of tourists. Late in the 1904 season, on 1 September, she was taking a party of sightseers to view the scenery at Lamorna Cove. An old sailor on board was enthralling the excursionists with the story of the *Lady*'s exploits during the disastrous wreck of the German mail liner *Schiller* at Scilly, when there was the sound of a low rumble under the bows as she grazed the sunken ledge of the Little Heaver, just off the edge of Carn-du. She was soon floated off but was then beached in the little cove, close by the pierhead, leaving her alarmed and somewhat dishevilled passengers to walk the four miles back to Penzance! Here she lay for a few days, at times submerged from bows to bridge, with three big holes below her engine room. A spell of fine weather spared her any further damage and the *Lady* was refloated by the Little Western Salvage Company, with the aid of a Falmouth tug, and towed back into Penzance. Her injuries were not too serious but, nevertheless, her owners decided that, in view of her age, it was not worth their while repairing her and she was sold to the salvage company. They had her re-boilered and fitted out as a salvage steamer, in which capacity she could boast of being present at every major wreck on the Cornish coast for the next thirty years.

The incident with the *Lady of the Isles* occurred some eighty five years after a previous Scilly packet, the *Lord Howe*, also got into difficulties near the same point. After leaving Penzance bound for St. Mary's on the morning of 16 July 1816, carrying both merchandise and passengers, the *Lord Howe* ran onto a rock off Kenmel Point, just past Mousehole. Although she quickly filled with water, the speedy attendance of a number of fishing vessels ensured that all the passengers were got off safely and they even managed to save most of the cargo. It was alleged that the entire crew were below having dinner at the time of the accident and had left the ship's boy alone at the helm!

Cornwall was blessed with a large number of photographers operating in the county from the latter part of the 19th century onwards, no doubt partly due to the number of visitors. As a result, there was generous coverage of the area, at a time when other parts of the country were not nearly so fortunate photographically. Vying with each other to an extent, to sell photographs and, after 1900, postcards to both locals and tourists, all manner of places and incidents were recorded. The views of the *Lady of the Isles* are a good example of this. The bottom two in particular were published as picture postcards and, indeed, copies would almost certainly have been bought by those on board at the time of the wreck, as a memento of their brush with disaster. Today, many of these cards are highly sought after by collectors.

The steam screw packet *Lyonesse* pictured leaving St. Mary's, Scilly Isles, sometime in the early years of the 20th century.

formation of a second company and the arrival of a second vessel. The West Cornwall Steamship Company was formed in 1871 in Penzance and chiefly consisted of shareholders in the West Cornwall Railway, who no doubt saw an upturn in railway passengers, and therefore profits, as a direct result. The Company purchased the *Earl of Arran*, an iron paddler built at Paisley in 1860, and re-registered her in Penzance.

Despite the fact that these were two separate companies, there was no competition and they ran complementary services, the *Little Western* acting as the main packet boat, with the *Arran* running services as required, plus excursions in between. This rather cosy arrangement persisted for the first few months until, ironically, the *Earl of Arran* was wrecked on the islands on 16 July 1872, due to some reckless running under an uncertified pilot. All passengers and their baggage were safely got off, before the paddler settled on a reef off Nor Nor Island and, despite hopes off salvage, became a total loss.

Less than three months later, the *Little Western* was also lost when, if the story is true, her master deliberately wrecked her on Wells Reef on 6 October, in a drunken rage at having missed out on a possible salvage job. It proved to be the end of the Scilly Isles Steam Navigation Company, although the West Cornwall Company were straight back into the fray with the wooden paddler *Guide*, chartered from Dartmouth. She ran the service for three years, being relieved by the *Queen of the Bay* in 1874.

The handsome *Queen of the Bay*, which began life as a Morecambe Bay excursion steamer, following her launch at Renfrew in 1867, was the last paddler to ply to the islands. She also sailed from Blackpool before, in 1874, coming to Penzance, being re-boilered by Harveys the following year. Like many of the Scilly boats, she had a lively career, rescuing ships and imperilled sailors, such as in 1875 when she towed the dismasted Liverpool clipper *Rydal Hall* into St. Mary's Sound from near the Seven Stones, as well as helping to maintain the service to the islands. She was eventually sold in 1885 to Cardiff owners and was badly damaged by fire in the Usk, near Newport, in May 1894, being sold as a wreck shortly after.

Finally, in 1875, there arrived the first purpose-built and perhaps the most famous Scilly packet, the *Lady of the Isles*. She was launched by Harveys of Hayle in 1875 and she served the islands for twenty nine years, before her mishap in Lamorna Cove in 1904 led to her being sold to the company that salvaged her. The treacherous coast and waters between Penzance and the Scillies ensured that she, too, had her fair share of adventure; none was more dramatic, however, than her introduction to such events in 1875, when the German liner *Schiller*, bound for Hamburg from New York, struck the Retarrier Rocks in thick fog. *Lady of the Isles* towed the lifeboat out to the scene of the disaster but the liner sank as they arrived and only about forty souls survived out of a total of 384 on board.

The *Lady* was joined on the Scilly run in 1889 by a second

A good profile view of *Scillonian*. Ironically, given that the name is now synonymous with the Scilly boats, it had been intended originally to call her *Queen of the Isles* but the name was already in use. *Scillonian* could carry up to 400 passengers, plus cargo, and her triple expansion engines could propel her along at a breezy 12 knots.

vessel, as a result of the continuing increase in trade. This was the twin-funnelled *Lyonesse*, launched in 1889 and also built by Harveys, a handsome and elegant vessel which was commanded for many years by the exceedingly rotund Captain Tiddy. As an example of how lucrative salvage work could be, the *Lyonesse* earned a highly respectable £1,250 in 1903 when she towed the Glasgow barque *Queen Mab*, complete with cargo of fustic, into St. Mary's harbour. However, she was in trouble herself a year later, being damaged when hit by the Whitehaven steamer *Fleswick*. *Lyonesse* was almost twice the size of her sister but, like the *Lady*, she too ended her career as a salvage ship, though in Irish waters, only returning to her birthplace at Hayle in 1928, to be scrapped.

An unusual view of the *Scillonian* in Penzance harbour, with the Trinity House Vessel *Satellite* moored in front, probably taken in the 1950s.

However, throughout all this period there was no one boat dedicated to the Scilly service. This all changed with the launch of the *R.M.S. Scillonian*, built by the Ailsa Shipbuilding Company of Troon, in January 1926. At last the Scilly islanders had their own ship. Her maiden voyage was rough and troublesome and did not bode well. Even the fresh water ran out on the long haul down from the Clyde and tea had to be brewed with condenser water. Yet, in the distinctive livery of white hull and buff funnel,

In June 1934, the *Scillonian* was dry docked with N. Holman & Sons, who had recently refurbished their shipyard and erected the green corrugated iron workshops which, over sixty years later, are still a familiar part of the Penzance waterfront landscape. This photograph shows her being warped into the dock.

Berthed appropriately alongside the Scilly packet *Lyonesse* is the third class gunboat *Argus*, which was bought in 1920 by the Isles of Scilly S.S. Company and renamed *Penninis*. She sailed as the mail packet until the arrival of *Scillonian* in 1926. Launched in 1904 by Bow McLachlan of Paisley, the vessel served as a fishery protection cruiser and, on 11 July 1906, she arrested the Paimpol (France) fishing boats *Fletan*, *Emeraude*, *Helene* and *Perle*, bringing them into Penzance where this photograph was taken. They were each fined £70, a substantial sum in 1906, and had their nets confiscated. Only a few days before, during the Royal Navy's spring manoevres, the *Argus* had anchored in St. Mary's Pool and, sending a cable into Portmellin, had supplied electricity by charging batteries for the Marconi station. Fishery protection vessels in those days were manned by reservists. In 1907, the master of the *Argus*, Warrant Officer William Hicks became the first reservist to be commissioned, as a Lieutenant R.N., which required a special Order in Council. The *Argus* itself became a Navy vessel during the war, her name being changed to *Argon* to avoid confusion with a ship of the same name. As *Penninis*, she was sold in 1927 to a Channel Islands company and renamed *Riduna*. She was broken up at Plymouth in 1932.

she was to nobly serve the islands in peace and war for the next thirty years.

Scillonian was ordered by the Isles of Scilly Steamship Company Ltd., formed in 1919 to takeover and improve services to the islands, as a result of the severe financial difficulties which the West Cornwall Company had been experiencing for a number of years. They first operated with the ex-fishery protection and Navy gunboat *Argus* (later *Argon*), bought in 1920, re-registered in the islands and renamed *Penninis*. This stylish looking craft ran the packet service for six years until the launch of *Scillonian* and her master, Captain MacAlister, then took over the new arrival.

Launched by Thorneycroft of Southampton, in the spring of 1956, *R.M.S. Scillonian II* would also spend thirty years running between Penzance and the islands. Much larger than her predecessor – she could carry 500 passengers and had two thirds more cargo capacity – she was ordered as a result of the first vessel's success in developing the burgeoning tourist trade to the islands. Like her past sisters, she too often stood by distressed ships and she also suffered her share of bad weather. Because of her larger size, she could struggle to enter the harbour at Penzance in poor conditions and, indeed, one particularly rough day in March 1959 saw her diverted as far as Falmouth, this being the nearest harbour capable of taking her which was not already full of sheltering craft. This led to a suggestion that the service be permanently diverted there but the understandable storm of protest from Penzance folk meant the idea was quickly dropped.

The main problem with running the service with a single vessel was one of relief, when *Scillonian II* was in drydock in Southampton for her annual overhaul. Over the years a number of craft from Poole and even coasters from Holland were used as temporary substitutes but the problem was finally solved in 1965 following the launch of the Company's own relief vessel, the *Queen of the Isles*. She was ordered from builders Charles Hill and Sons of Bristol and, in size, was more akin to the original *Scillonian*.

R.M.S. Scillonian III was the largest yet of the islands' ferries when she was launched by Appledore Shipbuilders in May 1977. Modern and well-equipped, she broke with the traditional company livery when she suddenly boasted a blue-banded funnel and sides. This generated much disapproval in the islands and she soon returned to normal colours, except for the funnel which still carries a representation of the house flag painted on by the author!

The bit they don't mention in the brochures! Another graphic illustration of the rough conditions that can be encountered as *Scillonian II* rolls alarmingly coming into Penzance harbour during a heavy south east gale in March 1963.

ISLES OF SCILLY STEAMSHIP COMPANY, LTD.

DAY TRIPS TO THE ISLES OF SCILLY

EVERY MONDAY, TUESDAY, FRIDAY AND SATURDAY

From June 21st, and until further notice, Weather and other circumstances permitting, and subject to the conditions of the Company's ordinary Sailing Bills

THE ROYAL MAIL STEAMER

"SCILLONIAN"

Will leave the LIGHTHOUSE PIER, PENZANCE, at **9.30 a.m.**, and start from the ISLES OF SCILLY on the return journey at **4.15 p.m.**

FARE: Return 20/-

(Children under 14 half-price).

For Other Sailings see Ordinary Sailing Bills.

Saundry, Printer, Chapel Street, Penzance. 'Phone 3401.

In September 1977, the author was outward bound on *Scillonian III* on his first ever trip to the Isles of Scilly, when she went to the aid of the French trawler *Kerland*, which was sinking off the Runnelstone buoy. Burdened by a large model ship, he was without his customary sketchbook but managed to record the subsequent rescue on the only available paper – brown paper bags usually employed for a far less pleasant task!

The little *Queen of the Isles*, launched at Bristol in 1965 as a relief boat for *Scillonian II*, pictured at Penzance refuelling in the late 1960s. In the 1970s, she was sold away to Fiji.

In 1989, the Swedish cargo ferry *Gry Maritha* exchanged the cold waters of the Baltic for the sunnier climes of the Scillies and south Cornwall, when she took over the islands cargo service. Launched in 1981 and named after the then Captain's small daughter, the *Gry Maritha* also acts as seasonal relief, plying to the islands when *Scillonian III* is laid up during the winter months.

From the earliest days of the Scilly Islands service, the packet boats have come to the aid of vessels – and seamen – in distress, a duty they will no doubt continue to perform without question. This striking photograph was taken in April 1966, as *Scillonian II* stood by when the small Dutch coaster *Saba*, of Groningen, capsized and sank off Porthgwarra, after her cargo of steel shifted in a hard SSW gale.

Launched at Appledore in 1977, *R.M.S. Scillonian III* is a most attractive looking vessel, as demonstrated in this purposeful pose taken at Penzance in the 1980s. Note the substantial electrically operated crane, forward, for her cargo carrying duties and the house flag of the Isles of Scilly Steamship Company painted on the funnel – the author's own work!

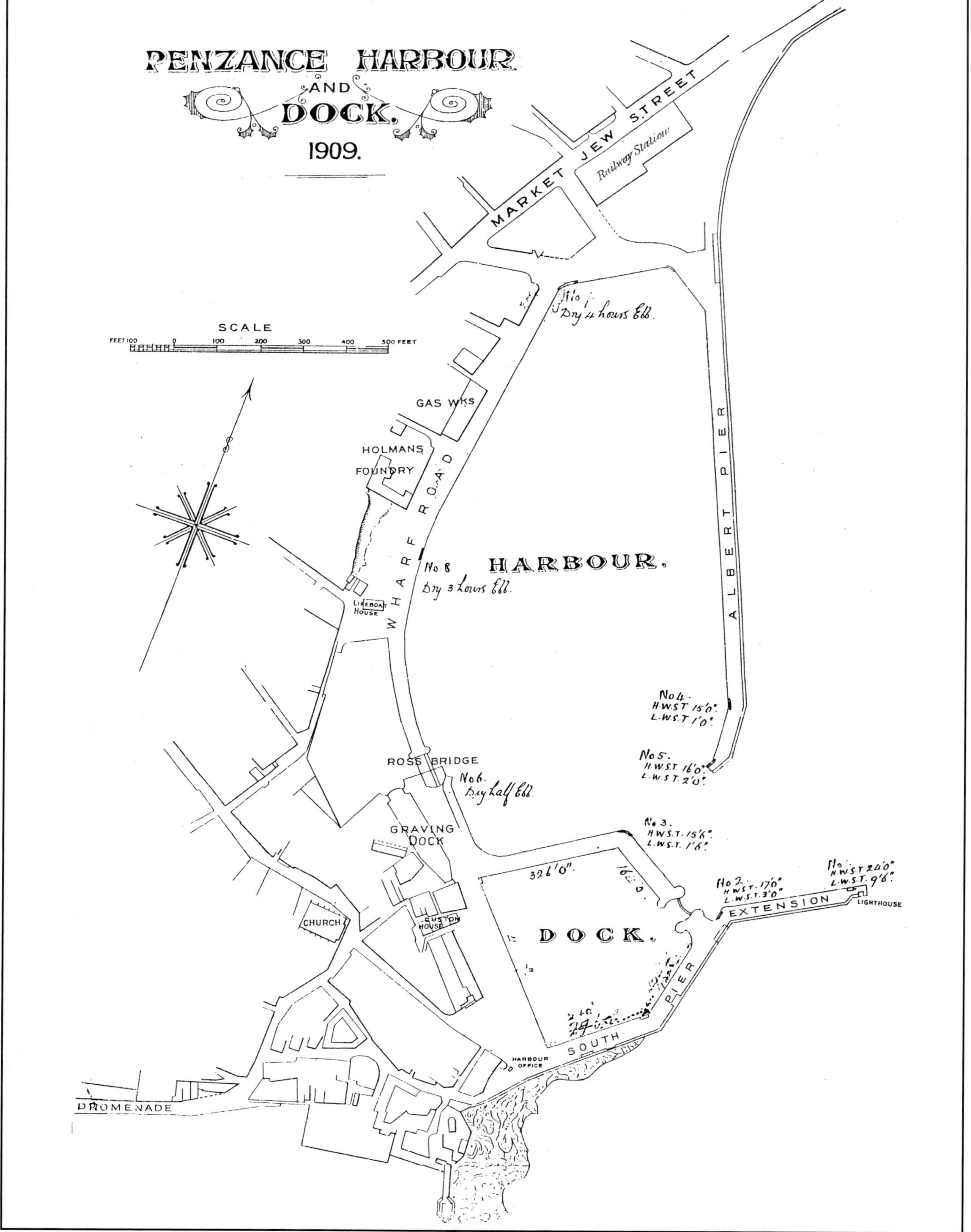
PENZANCE HARBOUR
AND
DOCK.
1909.
SCALE
FEET 100 0 100 200 300 400 500 FEET
MARKET JEW STREET
Railway Station
GAS WKS
HOLMANS
FOUNDRY
WHARF ROAD
No 7
Dry 4 hours Ebb.
No 8
Dry 3 hours Ebb.
HARBOUR.
ALBERT PIER
LIFEBOAT HOUSE
No 4.
H.W.S.T 15'0".
L.W.S.T 1'0".
No 5.
H.W.S.T. 16'0".
L.W.S.T. 2'0".
ROSS BRIDGE
No 6.
Dry half Ebb.
GRAVING DOCK
No 3.
H.W.S.T. 15'6".
L.W.S.T. 1'6".
326'0".
No 2.
H.W.S.T. 17'0".
L.W.S.T. 3'0".
No 1.
H.W.S.T 24'0".
L.W.S.T. 9'6".
EXTENSION
LIGHTHOUSE
CHURCH
CUSTOM HOUSE
DOCK.
PIER
SOUTH
HARBOUR OFFICE
PROMENADE

Chapter 4
The Halcyon Years of the Coasting Trade

'13 May. 50 tons coal landed on Dock side ex S.S. Coath. *300 barrels petroleum landed on Dock side ex ketch* Mizpah *for the Anglo American Oil Co. 15 May. 350 tons coal landed on Albert Pier ex* S.S. Volante *for Craske & Co. 100 tons coal landed on Albert Pier ex* S.S. Holman Sutcliffe *for Mr. Taylor.'* Penzance Dock Report Book 1912.

Prior to the building of the wet dock in the 1880s, vessels laid up on the mud in between tides and whilst awaiting cargoes. In this circa 1872 photograph, a Plymouth sailing trawler, one of many that came down for the season, lies beached out in the 'Gaps'. In the background, the town's schooner fleet can be seen sitting, at half tide, in the outer harbour, or lying alongside the Albert Pier.

Of all the ships heeled on the mud off the Albert Pier, or pointing their bowsprits towards the windows of the Dolphin Hotel, none were more distinctive or hard worked than the mining schooners. Most were owned by the powerful St. Just mining families in consortium with merchants, engineers and various genteel dabblers, such as schoolmasters and doctors. The schooner *Gazelle* often appeared in the coast books of the great Balleswidden tin mine, while the *Lafrowda* was one of the fastest. The Garibaldi-rigged *Prima Donna*, which came to Penzance in 1861, was partly owned by Edmund and Richard Davy who, besides being shareholders in many St. Just mines, ran a thriving brewery and coal yard in Jennings Street. They also owned the barque *Sir Humphrey Davy*, named after their famous scientific uncle, sending her to ports as far away as Calloa and Algoa Bay.

A view of the harbourside around 1871. A ship can be seen in the old dry dock, the entrance to which faces into the harbour, whilst just visible is the partly built hull of the ketch *Lady St. Aubyn*, which spent her life in the faraway Timor Sea. The line of ships includes the paddle tug *Wolf*, moored beside the small loading jetty used in the building of the Wolf Rock Lighthouse.

Other mining men with a taste for shipowning were the Boyns family who controlled Wheal Owles, Boswedden and St. Just United. To save on coal freights, 'Purser' Boyns had the schooner *Mary Boyns* launched for him in June 1858, her figurehead being the bust of his nephew Richard's wife Mary and after whom the vessel was named. Commanded by Captain John Dusting, she had a disastrous collision on her maiden voyage

For a period, from the time of the First World War until the late 1930s, Penzance was an important shipping point for china clay, transported to the quayside from the newly opened Leswidden pits, near St. Just, in horse-drawn carts, as well as Foden steam waggons. It brought much extra shipping to the port and also provided a good deal of manual labour.

and, though viewed with pride as she sailed past the St. Just cliffs, her career was not happy. The Mousehole fishermen swore that she brought gales with her and in May 1868 she was the unwitting spectator of the tragic wreck of the steamer *Garonne*, at Lamorna. Only a few months later she was the last to see the Looe mining schooner *Caradon*, which vanished off Newquay. The *Mary Boyns* was herself lost when, homeward bound with engine coal for Wheal Owles, she was rammed by the Whitby steamer *Mulgrave*, off Godrevy.

Captain John Dusting took over her successor, the smart iron schooner *Boswedden*, launched at Shields in December 1884 and, although one of the few Penzance ships adequately equipped with lifesaving gear, she vanished off Hartland in October 1886. All that came ashore was a brass bound bucket on Lundy and a writing desk, washed up near Ilfracombe. After this tragedy the 'St. Justers' forsook shipowning, while the Davy's retired and sold their *Prima Donna* to Captain Richard Holbrook, a Welsh mariner who settled in Penzance and later became harbour master. Edmund Davy died soon after the *Prima Donna* was swallowed by the Great Blizzard of March 1891, while homeward bound with coal for the Holbrook brothers' Triangular Stores in Barbican Lane.

The end of this great tradition was the *Lanisley*, a heavily rigged iron schooner launched by Harveys of Hayle in June 1887. She was well equipped with steam winches and roller reefing and, commanded by Captain Barzalai Beckerleg, outsailed even the crack *Lafrowda*. Yet the shadow of the *Mary Boyns* still lingered. At dawn on 19 October 1895, a farm labourer found Captain Beckerleg, lifebelt about his waist, jammed amongst the rocks at Westward Ho! He was near to death but his rescuers, mistakenly believing they were cut off by the tide, manhandled him over the rocks and through the surf to Ilfracombe lifeboat. Tragically, he died just as she reached harbour. He was buried at Penzance and his coffin was borne by fellow coasting captains Harry of the *Lafrowda*, Cattran of the *Mary Hannah*, Rosewall lately of the *Fenna & Willemina*, Morrish of the *Sappho*, James of the *Mary James* and Symons lately of the *Killiow*. There was bitter criticism of the Ilfracombe men such that, a few weeks later, a band of Penzance schoonermen went to Westward Ho and using a dummy equal to the captain's figure satisfied themselves he could have been carried up the cliff.

The *Lanisley* tragedy plunged Penzance into mourning but the winter was not over and on Christmas Eve the schooner *Pilgrim*, which had many times hauled the year's supply of coal for Madron Workhouse, went missing off Land's End. These lost crews were commemorated on a marble plaque in St. Mary's church but the gaps they left in the Penzance coasting fleet were never filled.

The heyday of sail was over and a lot of the coal traffic had already been captured by the steam colliers of James Henry Bennetts. Born in 1843, Bennetts was the son of a mason who had built the Queen's Hotel on the promenade. As a young man he had migrated to South Wales, working at the Park End Deep Colliery, near Maesteg, and learning the coal business from its

Coal was another important cargo shipped into Penzance. In this 1920s postcard view, the collier *Galacum*, of Partington, can be seen discharging into carts on the North Quay coal berth.

owners the Brogdens, who had operated steam colliers since the 1870s. Bennetts then graduated to the blast furnaces and steel mills of the Midlands, before returning home in 1882 to establish himself as a coal merchant and colliery agent. He soon bought the redundant Penzance coasting steamer *Progress* and then the iron collier *Ormerod*, which was commanded by Captain Tom Beckerleg, brother of the unfortunate Barzalai. Bluff and hearty, he was the epitome of the old time sailor and he too later became harbour master.

Beckerleg displayed his fine seamanship when, homeward bound from Liverpool in a heavy NNE gale, he was surprised to encounter, off the Smalls, the dismasted schooner *Fenna & Willemina* which, having been bought by Bennetts some months before, was bound for Bristol from Newlyn with roadstone. The *Ormerod*'s mate Arthur Downing, the steward Charlie Pezzack and A.B. Charlie Ash earned lifesaving medals for rowing the collier's boat through huge seas to save the schoonermen, while Cap'n Tom pumped out oil to calm the seas – one of the first times such a method had been used.

By 1900, Bennetts was a successful businessman supplying house, smithy, bunker and mine coal using the *Ormerod*, the *Vril* – the first steamer to use the new Holman drydock – and the small collier *India*, the vessel which was to spoil the excellent record of the company's busy and well run little fleet. On a clear night in April 1910, she was bound from Jersey to Weston Point with china stone when the lookout failed to recognise the lights of the Belgian tug *John Bull*, which was towing the Liverpool clipper *Kate Thomas* from Antwerp to Port Talbot. The *India* rammed the clipper on the starboard bows and, despite the fact that she was ten times the size of the little collier, in ten minutes

Part of what was Penzance's 'Sailorstown'; a 1930s photograph, looking up Church Street to St. Mary's, with the Dock Hotel on the left and Laity's general stores beyond.

Towering above the clay sheds, the Baltic barquentine *Elizabeth* was photographed loading china clay for Gothenburg in January 1924. Once down to her marks, she was towed out to sea by the steam trawler *Prince*, herself outward bound for the Morroccan fisheries.

The magnificent figurehead of William Ashburner, adorning the schooner of that name.

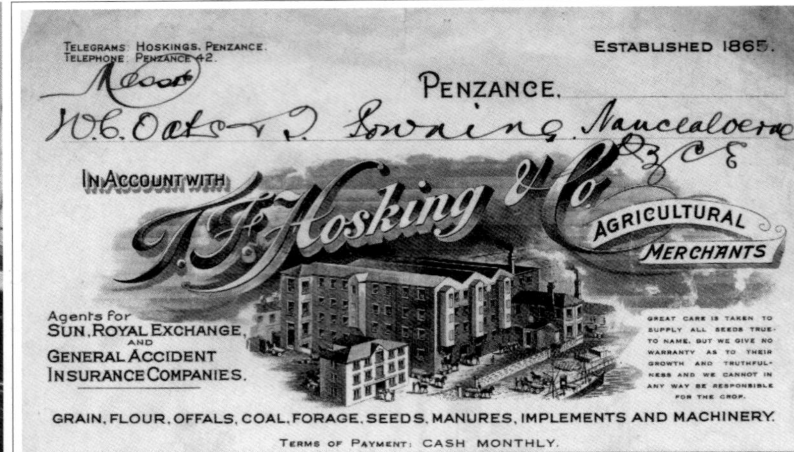

TELEGRAMS: HOSKINGS, PENZANCE.
TELEPHONE: PENZANCE 42.

ESTABLISHED 1865.

PENZANCE.

IN ACCOUNT WITH T. F. Hosking & Co. AGRICULTURAL MERCHANTS

Agents for
SUN, ROYAL EXCHANGE, AND
GENERAL ACCIDENT
INSURANCE COMPANIES.

GREAT CARE IS TAKEN TO SUPPLY ALL SEEDS TRUE TO NAME, BUT WE GIVE NO WARRANTY AS TO THEIR GROWTH AND TRUTHFULNESS AND WE CANNOT IN ANY WAY BE RESPONSIBLE FOR THE CROP.

GRAIN, FLOUR, OFFALS, COAL, FORAGE, SEEDS, MANURES, IMPLEMENTS AND MACHINERY.

TERMS OF PAYMENT: CASH MONTHLY.

The *William Ashburner* being towed out of the wet dock in ballast in 1938, possibly heading for the dry dock. The smoke visible to the rear comes from her auxiliary engine

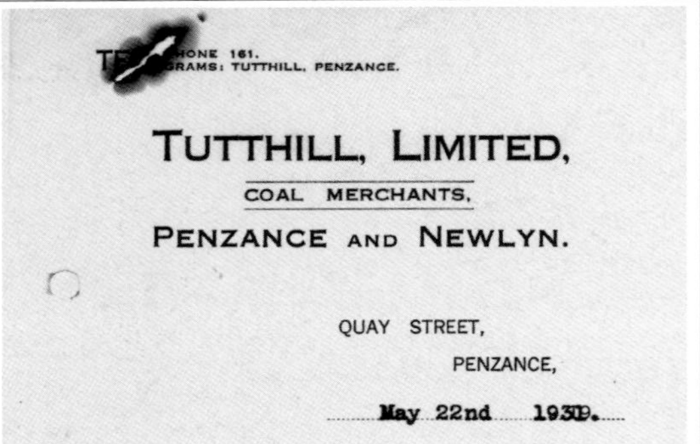

TE[illegible]HONE 161.
[illegible]RAMS: TUTTHILL, PENZANCE.

TUTTHILL, LIMITED,
COAL MERCHANTS,
PENZANCE AND NEWLYN.

QUAY STREET,
PENZANCE,

May 22nd 1939.

The Falmouth schooner *Mary Barrow*, having unloaded a cargo of bagged cement, backloads empty bags in the 1920s. Built in 1891, she was wrecked off the Calf of Man in 1938.

26 - 3 - 1939.

Mr T. Mitchell

BOUGHT OF

TELEGRAMS:- DUCHY, PENZANCE.
TELEPHONE Nº 24.

J.H.TONKING, L^TD

THE BOROUGH STORES

PENZANCE.

Some examples of letterheads, some of them beautifully ornate, for local businesses are shown on this page and others. All of these companies relied on the port for their supplies of coal and general goods until the Second World War and beyond.

A Dartmouth-registered small trading ketch discharges potatoes for Wm. Hall, forage and general merchants, on the Gas Wharf around 1930. This section of the harbour was filled in to make a car park in the 1950s.

ALBERT STREET,
PENZANCE, Feb 10 1892

Mr Harris Congregational Church

Bought of **JOSEPH DENLEY,**

COAL MERCHANT.

Jan 9 | 10 cwt coals @ 24/ | 0 12 0

Although a surprising number of old sailing coasters survived the war years, they were still so few as to be a rarity in Cornish ports and, from 1945, the sight of a ketch or schooner coming into port often created a bit of a stir. Here, the steel schooner *Eilian*, of Barnstaple, arrives with bunker coal from Cardiff on 28 August 1955. Launched at Amlwch, Anglesey, in 1908, as an auxiliary with a small parafin engine, she sailed out of Barnstaple for most of her life, until sold to Danish owners in October 1957. Opposite her is the M.V. *Fred Everard*, herself launched as a sailing barge in 1938. She had narrowly escaped being lost on her previous voyage, after striking the Welloe Rock, off Cuddlan Point. By the time of this photograph, the old clay sheds had become 'Thomas's Snack Bar' where, as a young art student, the author enjoyed many cups of appalling tea with the dockers and coal heavers.

she had heeled over and gone, leaving only a young apprentice as the sole survivor of a compliment on nineteen.

The *India* and the other two coal boats were eventually sold foreign and replaced by the collier *Sir Edward Bacon*, speedily renamed *Pivoc*, an anagram made up of the first letters from the names of previous ships Bennetts had owned. His rivals at Penzance included Sampson R. Taylor, who founded the Penzance Dry Dock & Coal Company and who ran the *Lucien*, an ancient French clipper steamer converted to a hulk, which was towed to and from Wales loading bunker coal for East coast steam drifting fleets. Craske & Co. of Lowestoft regularly sent down their own hulks, though Sterry and Co. operated a steam barge, the *Sterry*, which on her maiden trip would have been wrecked if a farmer had not bicycled to Porthleven with news that she was among the shoals of Rinsey Head.

The seaweed gatherers much frequented the old Yacht Inn and it was easy to know when they were at the bar as water from their sodden clothes ran out under the double doors. Quay Street still had plenty of pubs where the rule was that drunks, once thrown out, were always laid 'parallel with the gutter', to protect them from the wheels of passing coal carts and so to ensure they returned the next day. Fighting was part of the evenings entertainment, with the police often borrowing a hand cart to take away the combatants and one small boy remembered a black sailor, lurching out onto the cobbles, with a hatchet buried in the back of his head!

Although steam coasters and colliers now ran the big cargoes, there was still room for the last of the small sailing vessels to make a living. The old mining schooner *Golden Light* was the last vessel owned by William Calf & Sons, coal and general merchants. She was a well worn veteran which had escaped being wrecked at Padstow, driving ashore at Penzance and being posted missing during the Great Blizzard of 1891. Once sold, she hauled bunker coal for the Scilly packets and, sold again, sank off Lundy in February 1918. The tiny smack *Concord*, under Captain Edwin Pascoe, ran groceries between Porthleven and Plymouth for years until wrecked on the Triggs while inward bound in March 1900. She was succeeded by the clinker built ketch *Pirate,* among whose crew was an incredibly large Negro cook with a very touchy temper.

The iron collier *Ormerod*, owned by James Henry Bennetts, lies discharging coal on the Albert pier in the background, as the ancient ketch *Ceres*, of Padstow, idles into harbour around 1908. Launched in 1811 at Salcombe, the *Ceres* was an amazing 125 years old when her age finally caught up with her and she sank at anchor, off Baggy Point, in 1936.

Tutthill, a one time employee of Sterry, set up his own coal yards, including one on the Battery where a flight of steps led down into an old fort which, for some unknown reason, was stacked with tea-chests filled with ancient books and documents. He soon moved his office to the bottom of Quay Street which was still the centre of a miniature 'Sailorstown'; chandlers and ancient cottages, ballast dumps and net lofts stood side by side, and there were small groceries better known as 'Fly Cemetries'. The Seamans Bethel was in Barbican Lane and also the less dignified 'Fourpenney Doss House' where, according to legend, for less than the proper fee customers went to sleep hanging over a line, which was cut at 6am to ensure nobody overslept!

Still on the Plymouth run was the ketch *Lady Elizabeth*, owned by the Mathews family who built her at the drydock back

Most owners commissioned oil paintings of their vessels, to hang on home or office walls as testament to their success. This is the painting Bennett had done of his last vessel, the *Pivoc*. Her unusual name was an anagram of the first letters of previous ships he had owned.

in 1871. She regularly hauled barrels of naptha and gasoline for the newly built depot of the Anglo American Oil Company, until she caught fire in the Cattewater at Plymouth in January 1900. A fiery end also consumed the small ketch *Albatross,* owned by Captain Martyn 'Marty' Grenfell, which sank in a shower of exploding oil barrels in the Solent in August 1905. To replace her the Mathews family bought their last vessel, the ketch *Lodore*, an ex-North Sea fish carrier launched near Brixham in 1878.

Penzance also had a steamer line, founded, like H.T.P. at Hayle, in flour milling and groceries. George Bazeley was a prominent merchant and businessman who, in 1870, took over an old established family milling business. He built new mills at Gulval and Wherrytown, and leased the Albert Stores, which was also a mill, as well as a large grocery wholesale emporium. At first, Bazeley relied upon local ships but, believing that no ship was as profitable as one you own, he soon acquired the schooner *Beta*. Commanded by Captain William Beckerleg (brother of Tom and Barzalai), she hauled surplus flour to the family's new warehouses in Cardiff and brought back grain, groceries or coal for the steam mills.

Trade was so good that, in October 1877, their first steamer, the *Progress*, arrived at Penzance harbour. She had been bought to operate between London and Swansea with cargo and passengers, and William Beckerleg was given command. The response to the new service was overwhelming but the firm prudently waited eighteen months to be sure of their markets before buying a second steamer, the *W.J. Taylor*. She served them for barely a year before she was run down off Rotherhithe in November 1882; all on board gained the other vessel's bows, led by a sailor clutching a three month old baby boy travelling from Marazion to London for adoption. Fortunately for the Penzance shopkeepers, most of her cargo was consigned from Bristol to London and the resilient George Bazeley hired another steamer, the 405 ton *Stockton*. Within twenty four hours, she had brought down the cargo destined for the sunken *W.J. Taylor*. As a more permanent replacement, they tried the *Acacia* but she was unsuccessful, so the *Stockton* properly joined the fleet, now styled the Little Western S.S. Co. and carrying black funnels with a white 'B' on a red band.

To cope with increasing trade more ships were bought and, on 13 May 1884, the *Thames* was the first vessel to steam into the newly completed dock at Penzance. She was by then an old ship, launched in 1856 at Stockton-on-Tees, but she gave excellent service, as did others of her origin and vintage which Bazeley bought from the north country. Newer ships were added. In 1885 the 417 ton *Mercutio*, a five year old Mediterranean trader, arrived at Penzance but her debut was inauspicious; Bristol bound,she ran down the Newcastle collier *Edward Eccles* in the Avon and, in trying to avoid the accident, the Irish packet *Lady Woodhead* went onto the mud. Three days later, on her next upward trip, the *Mercutio* collided with the *City of Richmond* and reached Cumberland with a single bulkhead keeping her afloat.

It was not unusual for Bazeley's steamers to collect damage

It was a hard life coasting, so it is little surprise that it attracted or created hard men. Schedules had to be kept and cargoes delivered on time and, in any case, after a round trip of a few weeks, the crew were often anxious to get home. It was not unusual, therefore, for chances to be taken with the weather. The mainly Cornish crew of the Cardiff collier *Porthminster*, seen leaving Penzance on a rough day in April 1939, would probably have thought little of these conditions. The *Porthminster*'s sister vessels, *Porthcarrick* and *Porthmear*, were also regular callers at the harbour.

Although the negative is now unfortunately in poor condition, the historic nature of this photograph merits its inclusion. It shows the Norwegian steamer *Noordvag*, of Christiansand, bound for Philadelphia, with the largest cargo of china clay ever shipped from Penzance on 17 June 1922. Many people came out to watch her depart, as she was a rather tight fit in the wet dock and had to inch her way out very carefully, as can be seen from the picture.

Empty wooden flower boxes being unloaded on the quay for shipping to the Scilly Isles. They would return crammed with fresh flowers, to be whisked off to Covent Garden by express train and on sale within 24 hours of being picked.

There were many boats which became regular callers over the years and even when one stopped coming – lost, scrapped or sold on – others soon took its place in local affections. The *Oakford*, a fairly standard small steam collier, was often to be seen in the harbour prior to WW1, delivering coal to Penzance laundry or one of the local merchants.

For over fifty years cargoes of boxwood, for the flower industry, were regularly landed at Penzance, from vessels such as the Baltic steamer *Orion*, photographed here discharging wood from Tallinin on 15 April 1938.

Outward bound in ballast for Par, the small motor coaster *Robrix*, of Hull, sails from Penzance after unloading artificial manure for Coast Lines Limited on 1 February 1932.

in the busy river waters they visited on every voyage. To repair them, Bazeley had his own smithy at Penrose Terrace, close to the Albert Stores and, in July 1882, he clashed with the Town Council regarding a new wooden wall for the building, which was considered to be a fire risk. In the course of the argument, he drew attention to the service he was rendering with his business and the bringing down of the Garston steamers, which loaded greens and new potatoes for the busy Midland markets, and landed coal for the glasshouse growers and market gardeners.

George Bazeley died in December 1886 and his sons continued the expansion of the fleet, which now supplied the town with everything from embossed wallpaper to barrels of stout and from billycock hats to patent manure. Their weekly service ran like proverbial clockwork, apart from minor collisions. Only one Little Western ship was lost, the *Thames*, London bound on 2 January 1891, when she grounded on Chesil Bank in thick fog. A less serious 'loss' was the *Stockton*, one of the imaginary casualties 'sunk' by the gunboat *H.M.S. Leda* on an excercise in which she 'shelled' Penzance harbour and stormed the coastguard station in a hail of blank rounds, much to the delight of the local boys, in April 1888.

By the turn of the century, the Little Western fleet comprised two erstwhile members of the Clyde S.S. Co., the 400 ton steel coaster *Coath* and the 500 ton *Cloche*, the elderly *Gervaise* and the even older *Albert*, soon to be sold to Fowey owners. The *Gervaise*, after twenty one years service, went to the Russians in 1906 and the Little Western S.S. Co. themselves were taken over by Coast Lines Limited in 1920.

Then there was the Denley family of Penzance. Father, son and grandson, all named Joseph, the Denleys were coal, corn and general merchants who also dealt in secondhand ships gear and scrap metal, at the Marine Stores in Albert Street. They also ran a small fleet, mostly salvage prizes like the brigantine *Providence*, formerly the *Otto* until she drove onto the Eastern Green. She was commanded by Captain Robert Eastaway, a '*regular old shellback, with every hair on his head like spun yarn*'. The *Providence* plied to Wales and the Baltic alongside the other Denley ships. In 1876, they acquired an ex-Frenchman, the *Alexandre* and, when she was lost at Porthcawl, the Denleys went to another auction and bought the Paimbeouf Icelander *St. Joseph*, which a had propensity for collisions.

The *St. Joseph* was to prove their worst buy; even at the time of purchase, she was lying half-demolished after a collision off the Wolf. Then, on 19 February 1885, she hit the Fowey

The Liverpool coaster *Pink Rose* arrives with coal from Blyth, on the north east coast, in August 1939. Originally named *Pansy*, she was always referred to by the Penzance dockers as the 'Pansy Rose'. She was a regular caller at the port until bombed in the Irish Sea a couple of years after this photograph was taken.

PENZANCE STEAM FLOUR MILLS.

190

M

Bot. of R. M. Branwell & Sons.

John Joseph Uren, mariner, artist and master sailmaker, posing in his loft with the canvas wheel cover of the *William Ashburner* in 1932. Born in 1865 and one of thirteen children, he went to sea at the age of ten as an apprentice sailmaker and subsequently sailed twelve times round the world in ships like the Liverpool square rigger *Cromdale*, the New Zealand clipper *Piako* and Devitt & Moore's famous Australia-run clipper *Macquarrie*. John Joseph even had a medal for lifesaving, for rescuing a man from drowning in Devonport dockyard around 1900. By the 1920s, he had established a sail making business in the top loft of what is now the Penzance dry dock offices. He remained a highly capable 'sail and canvas man' and once had the job of making up a 'Big Top' for the Bertram Mills Circus. He was an excellent amateur painter and became a great friend of the Newlyn school artist Stanhope Forbes, who painted him in his loft as 'The Sailmaker'.

schooner *Rebecca* off Tol-pedn. She was finally lost in a third collision when she drove her bowsprit into a Cardiff tug which was trying to drag her clear of Penarth Head. The tug was unable to hold her and the *St. Joseph* drifted ashore where she was smashed up. By then, the Denleys had bought what was to be their last vessel, the *Chrysolite*, a replacement for the dandy *Alliance*, wrecked behind the Albert Pier on 9 December 1886.

The *Chrysolite* began life as a big, square-sterned Cumberland brigantine, launched at Whitehaven in 1869 and, at 159 tons, the largest vessel the Denleys ever owned. She was aquired by them after putting in following a bad collision off Longships. Sometime in her career she had been rerigged as a schooner and given a 'pole mizzen' mast but she remained a handsome vessel. She was not over fast but a sturdy and reliable vessel, painted black above the strake and tarred below, with the insides of her bulwarks white and the covering boards blue; around her hull was a gold line which, as customary in time of mourning, was painted blue. The *Chrysolite* also had the distinction of being the last Penzance vessel to carry a square sail. She was commanded from 1907 by Captain 'Marty' Grenfell and Billy Johns was the mate, while the cook was his brother Ned, who was to be drowned when the Penzance steamer *Coath* was mined in 1916. The third hand was 'Yankee Jack', a pleasant sailor who was later killed falling into a steamer's hold at Rotterdam.

A young Bideford sailor, who in 1911 arrived at the port onboard the Bude ketch *May Queen*, loaded with bricks and tiles from Bridgwater, sailed on a number of these vessels. Having met his future wife, he then shipped onboard the *Lodore*, referred to like the other vessels in this trade as a 'Grocery' ketch, his first job being to help scrape and paint the vessel. She was a surprisingly fast ship, '*stiff as a house and could run home from Plymouth often in under six hours*'. After a few trips he came ashore, as the captain's brother wanted a berth, but the *Lodore* was in a short while hulked, after being put on the gridiron at Plymouth.

The young sailor's next ship was the *Chrysolite*, which he joined in 1912 and which he still fondly recalled when talking to the author sixty years later. The *Chrysolite* regularly hauled culm from Neath and Briton Ferry for the Chyandour tin smelter. Sometimes, there was house or bunker coal from Cardiff, for the Denleys, while outwards there might be cargoes of roadstone, scrap metal from shipwrecks or tin slag for a glass works near Bristol, although such 'back cargoes' were inevitably scarce.

The young Bideford sailor and his comrades were the very last of the traditional schoonermen at Penzance. Captain 'Marty' was paid five pounds a month and the young

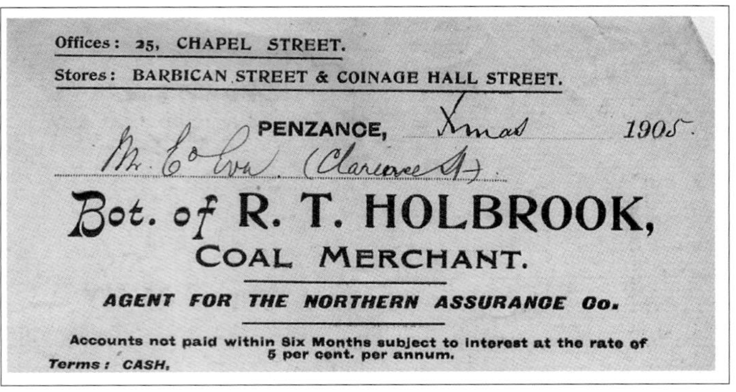

Offices: 25, CHAPEL STREET.
Stores: BARBICAN STREET & COINAGE HALL STREET.

PENZANCE, Xmas 1905.

Bot. of R. T. HOLBROOK,
COAL MERCHANT.

AGENT FOR THE NORTHERN ASSURANCE Co.

Accounts not paid within Six Months subject to interest at the rate of 5 per cent. per annum.
Terms: CASH.

sailor got three pounds fifteen shillings (£3.75), plus one and eightpence (8p) a day food allowance when in port. Late in 1912, the *Chrysolite* returned home on a voyage to find that the Chyandour smelter had shut and her crew were out of a job. She was sold away to Whitstable owners, the last schooner to sail out of Penzance and departed so quickly the young Bideford sailor had scarcely time to collect his gear from her. She was posted missing, believed run down by the steamer *Geraint*, off Morte Point, while bound from Cardiff to Treguier on 3 August 1918.

From the twenties onwards and until the demise of the British merchant marine, the quays at Penzance were dominated firstly by the tall smoking funnels of steam coasters and later by the rhythmic beat of diesel engines, of the new motor coasters. On every tide there was the rattle and clank of winches, as their holds disgorged house, gas and bunker coal which, as the century drew on, was more often hauled away by motor lorries, replacing the old horse drawn waggons.

The once thriving traffic in mine coal had drastically shrunk with the near end of mining at St. Just and a lack of cargoes forced James Henry Bennets to sell the *Pivoc*, his last vessel and, indeed, the last to carry 'PENZANCE' under her counter. She was wrecked in the estuary of the Seine in January 1922, just a few months before Bennetts himself died in London. His Company, however, remained the largest of the coal importers in the south west and, as consular and Lloyds Agents, was to be a mainstay of the harbour for the next seventy years.

A new export from Penzance, which was to bring extra shipping into the harbour, was china clay from the Leswidden pits, where a new works had been started alongside the famous Ballswidden tin mine, near St. Just. The clay was hauled to the quays by Foden steam waggons, whose drivers filled large water bottles, added cocoa and sugar and placed them next to the boilers, ensuring a hot drink was always at hand on a cold winter's morning.

On 13 December 1916, the schooner *Janie* loaded the first cargo of clay from the new concrete sheds which had been erected opposite the 'Dolphin'. The clay was stored here and loaded onto ships by means of a steam crane hoisting an iron tub, until replaced by an electric elevator. Penzance Council even proposed building a special jetty for the clay ships, to prevent the white dust billowing over the harbour, although this was used to advantage when the clay sheds became the waterfront at Marrakech during the making of a film in 1935; indeed, one local deliveryman was hired to drive his donkey cart around the quays whilst disguised as a Moroccan trader! By the time F. & T. Everard's motor coaster *Asperity* took the last cargo in May 1937, over 200,000 tons had been exported from Penzance.

Despite all this, it was a rough trade with little profit and there were constant complaints from consignees about water getting into the cargo, usually through leaking hulls in aged vessels, or broken hatches during stormy trips. In February 1927, the ancient ketch *Lucy* of Plymouth took a month to come down from Rochester, trailing in the wake of the schooner *Mary Barrow*. Launched back in October 1891 by W.H. Lean of Falmouth, for the Rio Grande trade (the import of animal hides for tanning, as well as hooves and bones which were boiled down for glue), the *Mary Barrow* was one of the first old sailing coasters regularly hauling Medway cement into Penzance. Her crew were equally old, including the mate who had served deep sea on the famous clipper *Thomasina McClellan*. The *Mary Barrow* remained in the cement trade until wrecked on the Calf of Man in 1938.

Two views of Coast Lines *Norfolk Coast* unloading seed potatoes at the West Quay in the 1930s.

Another schooner, the *S.F. Pearce*, had discharged cement across Mount's Bay at Porthleven on 22 October 1928 when, having sailed in a freshening southerly gale, she was almost driven ashore. Her crew started the engine but it soon failed and she spent a dangerous few hours jammed under Trewavas Head, before eventually they got it going again and motored clear of the rocks.

Another fondly remembered old schooner was the *William Ashburner* of Barrow, which was latterly owned and operated by the Kearon brothers, master and skipper, a pair of hard-fisted Irishmen from County Arklow. The *William Ashburner* made nearly fortnightly trips to Penzance with cement for Harvey & Co. If a cargo of clay was not available, she back-loaded bundles of empty cement sacks or had a spell in Holman's drydock.

In bad times she spent months laid up alongside the Albert pier, where her magnificent figurehead of William Ashburner was a source of wonder to small boys swimming in the harbour. Two Penzance lads even stowed away on her one time and had to be collected by the police at Plymouth. Another ran away to sea as a boy cook on the old schooner, at the time bound for Waterford to load potatoes for William Hall, who kept a large stores on Wharf Road. The lad soon learned to boil potatoes, fry bacon and plaster bread with margarine, the

Monmouth Coast at Penzance in the 1930s. She was part of the large Coast Lines fleet, whose vessels came to be well known at Penzance after the First World War and through to the early fifties, calling several times a week on their regular coastal runs between London and Liverpool.

traditional sailors fare, despite the vessel heavy rolling on the rough trip back home.

A worse job was being sent down into the hold to trim the cargo. Every time the schooner heeled before the wind, bags of potatoes fell over to one side. The lad would laboriously restack them and reset the shifting boards, only to have the same thing happen again when the vessel went onto the opposite tack. He was not very adept, either, at getting food from the galley to the cabin, which often earned him a clip round the ear. He received an even harder knock when the schooner's engineer enticed him into calling the Kearons something deeply insulting in Irish; years later, as a vigorous young sailor and champion boxer, he repaid the engineer in the bar of a pub in Penzance but, for now, he collected his wages and quit the decks of the *William Ashburner* for good.

After the First World War, the general cargo trade into Penzance was taken over by Coast Lines Limited, whose steamers called several times a week on their runs between Liverpool and London. In November 1922, they built the long sheds on the quay opposite the Trinity Depot and their brass nameplate remained on the double doors for years after the Company stopped calling.

By the 1920s, the old Victorian sailor town of Penzance was rapidly vanishing, victim of the manic desire to modernise, which would see a disastrous repetition thirty years later. A new civic gardens and bathing pool obliterated the historic buildings around the Battery, apart from the handsome Seamen's Mission which had been built in 1908, some years too late for the heyday of the port. The advent of chain stores banished what was left of the courts of cottages between Market Jew Street and the harbour, and even the seaweed gatherers had to find a new berth when the old Yacht Inn was replaced by a brand new pub of the same name.

Most of the old schoonermen and deepwater boys had long ago 'crossed the bar', often with a sad epitaph. Captain David Stevens had gone to sea when the Albert Pier was being built, onboard the Quebec emmigrant ships, and had been wrecked onboard the clipper barque *Lady Peel* in the St. Lawrence but when he died in October 1922 it was commented that '*His contempories are long since dead and almost forgotten*'.

Some of the old 'shellbacks' held what must have been a farewell dinner at the Dolphin Inn in January 1926. Among them was Tom Crocker, who had gone to sea at eleven onboard the schooner *Killiow*, of Penzance, and before he was fourteen rounded the Horn onboard the barque *Thomas Daniel*, commanded by Captain Bryant of St. Ives. One old sailor served on Mathews' brig *Prince Albert* and two others recalled living for a fortnight in a pipe, after being trapped in the port of Cette by the outbreak of the Franco Prussian War.

Only a week or so later came the death of Captain William Beckerleg, brother of Cap'ns Tom and Barzalai, who had risen to be a Commodore with the Hain Line and, though blind in later years, regularly put to sea in a pretty yacht crewed by the young Bideford sailor from the *Chrysolite*. Many of the veterans present at the dinner had helped man the famous old lifeboat *Elizabeth & Blanche*, which was even then being refitted for a round the world voyage under Captain George Hitchens, himself an erstwhile Hain Line Captain. He had bought her from Philip Nicholls, the last of the old time lifeboat coxswains, who had not only led the rescues in the surf at Longrock but had invented several fitments for the *Elizabeth & Blanche* and, as a Trinity pilot, had piloted the Royal Yacht *Britannia* when King Edward VII visited the Bay in 1908.

By the thirties, most of the pubs had gone from Quay Street and the 'roughness and toughness' was mostly limited to New Street, where every boy had his own tin bath to paddle around Abbey Basin looking for prizes among the moored ships. The Saturday night tradition of 'six policemen and a hand cart' was preserved though, largely thanks to one huge fisted individual, whose bosom companion created astonishment one day when he backed a pony and trap off the Albert Pier and, on landing upright, casually drove away. There was another equally eccentric character, who specialised in jumping from the cross trees of visiting schooners and was undetered when, at too low a tide, he fell and buried his head in the harbour lug sand! This last bastion of individuality and much of the old time port was soon to disappear.

Chapter 5
War in the Bay

'11.45 Tunisia *CNCZ AAAA 53.53N 19.02W . . . . sinking. 12.08 Port boats away. Starboard lifeboats smashed. Jolly boat now away.*' Land's End Radio transmission received from *S.S. Tunisia* 4 August 1941.

The 19th century British navy was characterised by the livery of the ships, in an age where the value of camouflage had not yet been appreciated. This turn of the century view shows an unidentified cruiser of the Victorian age at rest off Penzance, during summer manouevres, resplendent in her colours of black hull, white superstructure and buff funnels.

Many schoonermen, collier sailors and fishermen had, in the lean years before World War One, chosen to make extra pay by joining the Royal Naval Reserve. The Navy had always used Mount's Bay during the summer exercises of the Home and Channel fleets, although the elegant black hulls, white bridges and buff funnels of the Victorian navy was slowly replaced by battleship grey as a livery for visiting warships.

Much of the change was down to Admiral Sir Percy Scott, who revolutionised the British Navy when he took over as Admiral of the Fleet from Lord Charles Beresford. Under Beresford, appearance mattered far more than ability. Captains competed with each other to present their ships in immaculate style, often spending a small fortune on paint and polish, particularly the white enamel with which the bridge and superstructure were coated. Unfortunately, it tended to crack if the guns were fired and so gunnery practice was virtually nil. Admiral Scott's new Officer in Charge of Gunnery instigated a test firing shortly after assuming his position and was horrified to find an accuracy figure of barely fifteen per cent being attained. Fortuitously, Scott's reforms dragged the navy into the twentieth century, just in time for the outbreak of war.

The crews of the battleships *Monarch* and *Orion* march along the harbour front in honour of the King's birthday in June 1914, a few weeks before the outbreak of WW1.

In June 1914, the battleships *Monarch* and *Orion* anchored off Penzance. Next day, to celebrate the King's birthday, they both sent ashore large detachments which marched along the harbour front, the sailors and marines marching with fixed bayonets, and the entourage complete with maxim guns, ambulance party and naval band.

Barely eight weeks later, the waterfront again echoed to the sound of marshall music when, in August 1914, naval reservists marched to the railway station behind a band playing 'Hearts of Oak', to join special trains laid on by the G.W.R. bound for Portsmouth and Devonport. Some men soon found themselves in the turrets, stokeholds and gun casements of the same armoured

Another view of a fleet visit but also showing the Battery with its ancient guns. During the Second World War, 4.5 inch naval guns were installed, the first time that active armoury had been in place here since the wars against the French, nearly 200 years earlier.

cruisers and battleships which had so recently anchored in the early summer sunshine off Penzance and the Mount.

Soon, letters were arriving home telling of heroic deeds on the high seas. The son of the caretaker of the sports ground was onboard the cruiser *Highflyer* when she sank the German raider *Karlsruhe*, which in turn had chased the *S.S. Ortona*, commanded by Captain Barrett of Penzance. By the winter of 1914, eighteen reservists from the town were serving onboard everything from battleships to armed yachts.

There were inevitably casualties; a young marine was lost when the three cruisers *Aboukir*, *Hogue* and *Cressy* were sunk off the Dutch coast on the same day, barely a few weeks into the war in September 1914. Worse was to follow. In November, a small British cruiser squadron was destroyed off Coronel, on the Chilean coast, a region whose blistering nitrate ports had been visited by hundreds of Cornish sailors in peacetime. Among the ships lost was the *Monmouth*, the crew of which contained scores of Cornish coastguards and reservists including a young stoker who, until recently, had worked on the docks at Penzance. Another lost was Mousehole Coastguard Coleman Wright. Over thirty years later, his widow had her ashes scattered in the sea over the sunken cruiser from a Panamanian freighter.

Another battleship with a large Cornish contingent was the *Majestic*. She was torpedoed in the Dardanelles in May 1915 but, happily, most of the local reservists on board survived, including engine room artificer Frank Allen. The following Christmas, while serving onboard *H.M.S. Valiant* at Scapa Flow, he sent home seasonal greetings on the back of a postcard depicting the lost vessel!

Throughout the war, Penzance dock was crowded with naval launches, minesweeping trawlers and patrol drifters. Coastwise convoys rendezvoued behind long anti submarine booms but boatloads of torpedoed sailors often rowed into harbour. Everything from Cunard deckchairs to bales of Malayan rubber and dead American army mules were washed ashore. The big P. & O. liner *Ballarat* slipped stern first into thirty fathoms of water outside Penzance, sill loaded with gold bars worth ten

An historic photograph and a sight rarely seen beyond Spithead; the might of the combined Home and Channel Fleets assembled in Mount's Bay late in July 1910. In the harbour a couple of three-masted vessels, a barque and a barquentine, can be seen alongside and also a steam coaster, whilst, on the right, the dry docks and gasworks are prominent. On the far left, a small steamer is loading excursionists, no doubt taking them for a closer look at the warships. Immediately above her in the picture, is the salvage vessel *Greencastle*.

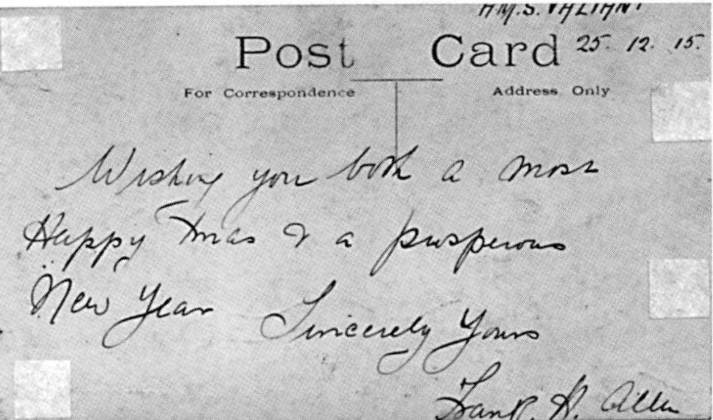

H.M.S. VALIANT

Post Card 25. 12. 15.

For Correspondence | Address Only

Wishing you both a most Happy Xmas & a prosperous New Year Sincerely Yours

Frank H. Allen

Engine room artificer Frank Allen's postcard home to Penzance at Christmas 1915. Sent from Scapa Flow, where the fleet spent much of the war, he had survived the sinking of the *Majestic* in the Dardanelles, seven months earlier.

This graphic commercial postcard, published by Cozens of Portsmouth just after the incident, illustrates the disastrous attack on the three 'Bacchante' class cruisers *H.M.S. Aboukir*, *Hogue* and *Cressy*, by the German submarine *U.9*, off the Dutch coast on 22 September 1914. They were all torpedoed and sunk, with inevitable loss of life, amongst them a young marine who had left Penzance only a matter of weeks before.

An erstwhile foe arrives at Penzance; *U.101*, only a year out of the Vulkan shipyard at Bremerhaven, is brought into the harbour under tow from Falmouth for scrapping, in January 1919. In an area which had suffered much, in terms of both men and ships lost to the U-boat menace, sights such as this were very welcome, giving local people a feeling of just revenge, as well as providing much needed work and income for local scrappers. *U.101* was broken up by J.H. Slade, whose premises were in Wharf Road and one of whose billheads is reproduced below.

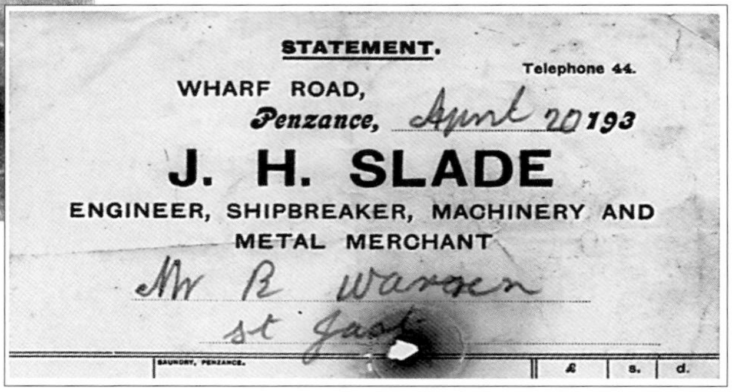

STATEMENT.

Telephone 44.

WHARF ROAD,
Penzance, April 20 193

J. H. SLADE

ENGINEER, SHIPBREAKER, MACHINERY AND METAL MERCHANT

Mr R Warren
St Just

A Naval motor launch fighting through heavy seas around Mount's Bay in 1914. These craft were built to operate in extreme conditions like this, as the weather did not prevent U-boats from patrolling.

Photographed under refit in the Holman dry dock in 1918 was *M.L. 352*, one of the large class – running to several hundreds – of fast 20-knot launches, built by the Elco Boat Building Company of New Jersey, U.S.A., for the Royal Navy. Sporting a 3-pounder gun and carrying a good supply of depth charges, they were used extensively on anti U boat operations around Mount's Bay.

million pounds.

World War One also took its toll on shipping around the Cornish coast, not least in the vicinity of Penzance. By the end of the U-boat war in 1918, a trail of sunken steamers stretched across Mount's Bay. Everything from gold bars to diplomatic secrets lay within the 20 fathom line. Off the Wolf Rock, a diver sank knee deep in a gulley filled with mercury, while near the Runnelstone, divers boots scuffed through millions of Rumanian machine gun bullets. Some found shell cases as tall as themselves, though they gave a wide berth to the massive jars they found filled with fulminate of mercury.

The patrol boats and minesweepers returned to Penzance in 1939 and, for the first time since the wars against the French, guns were mounted on the Battery, by the bathing pool, though these were now 4.5 inch, while Bofors guns and searchlights covered the approaches to the port from the Promenade. Sea traffic was normal during the first few days; the coasters *Moss Rose* and *Macville* discharged coal for J.H. Bennetts and the Co-Op, the yacht *Careen* arrived on a belated cruise from Dartmouth and the ketch *Result* landed a part cargo of cement from London. On the morning the latter sailed for Plymouth, the old *William Ashburner*, still under the Kearon brothers, arrived with cement and was still lying alongside when the schooner *S.F. Pearce* brought in another cargo. These old coasters remained on the coast until the Luftwaffe offensive in the spring but, in the meantime, the October gales arrived. The Portreath collier *Florence Reynolds*, deputising for the dry docked *Scillonian*, rode out a hard south easter off Sennen, when the reservists onboard declined the offer to return to Scilly.

The Irish auxiliary schooner *Loch Ryan* shows the results of the attack near Land's End by three Heinkel He 113s, in June 1940. It was a lucky escape for vessel and crew – she was shot to pieces and there were three unexploded bombs buried in her soft cargo of china clay but she managed to limp into Penzance harbour.

The Eastern beach and the vulnerable railway line were protected by pill boxes, barbed wire and anti invasion defences; the beach was also mined, although this hampered the rescue of the crew of a Whitley Bomber which crash landed in the shallows at Longrock. The port and drydock were taken over by the Royal Navy and, from July 1940, all coastwise shipping was rigidly controlled; every ship had to have a sailing permit and none could move between sunrise and sunset without the express permission of an S.N.O. (Senior Naval Officer), while her gunners had to remain at readiness to help the port's own A-A guns. Fishing boats and pleasure craft were subject to stringent fuel rationing, had to stay inside a two mile limit and were forbidden to speak with neutral ships.

Unlike the summer of 1915, the U-boats stayed well offshore and, apart from atrocious winter weather, the harbour was almost normal. Some of the old sailing coasters were still about and the *S.F. Pearce* used a calm spell to discharge cement, before going over to Falmouth where there was a stark reminder of the dangers faced by all ships; the bows of the tanker *Coroni River*, mined just the previous day. The old ketch *St. Austell* landed coal for Penzance Laundry, trundling around Land's End despite prowling bombers and completely unaware that a U-boat attack was going down. Survivors from the action arrived at Penzance behind the *St. Austell*.

Another crew came after the steamer *Polycarp* was torpedoed on 31 May 1940. The experience of 'Harry', her radio operator, was typical. With the captain and officers, he remained onboard after the steamer was abandoned. He sent out the 'SSSS' denoting submarine attack but the aerials had been damaged; the *Polycarp* began to sink very fast and they were all sucked down to a considerable depth. On surfacing, they swam away and a boat eventually picked up six of them. They hoisted sail and made for the land and were picked up by a French steamer which had already rescued the crew from another boat.

On arrival off Penzance, they went back into the boats and were towed in by a harbour launch. An ambulance was already waiting to take the injured to hospital and two buses to ferry the others to a hotel. Next day they were '*re-kitted with the bare neccessities at Simpsons of Penzance*' and those fit enough were soon on their way to Liverpool. At Truro the platforms were crowded and roads around the station were packed with troops who had been evacuated by small craft from northern France. These people were in various stages of exhaustion, many without kit; they comprised not only elements of the B.E.F. but also French, Belgian and Dutch soldiers.

With the onset of early summer, the lengthening days brought the Luftwaffe back into the skies above west Cornwall, opposed by only weakly armed convoy escorts and sporadic fighter patrols. Nothing was safe. Even the Seven Stones Lightship was strafed, while the *T.H.V. Satellite* was twice attacked off the Wolf Rock; after those incidents, she unshipped her mainmast in order to accommodate a 12-pounder gun. Neutral shipping did not go unscathed either, as the crew of the Irish auxiliary schooner *Loch Ryan* discovered. Bound from Par to Dublin with china clay, she was attacked shortly after leaving port by three Heinkels, which ignored the big Irish tricolour emblazoned on her sides. She crept in to Penzance with her sails cut to ribbons by machine gun fire and three unexploded bombs buried deep in her clay cargo.

There would be many more such attacks that summer and the shortening days also brought back the Heinkel minelayers. Under cover of the autumn gloom, they parachuted mines into the approaches of ports, even those as small as Penzance. A gang of small boys playing on the battery amused themselves by throwing stones at a strange object; it was hit several times before

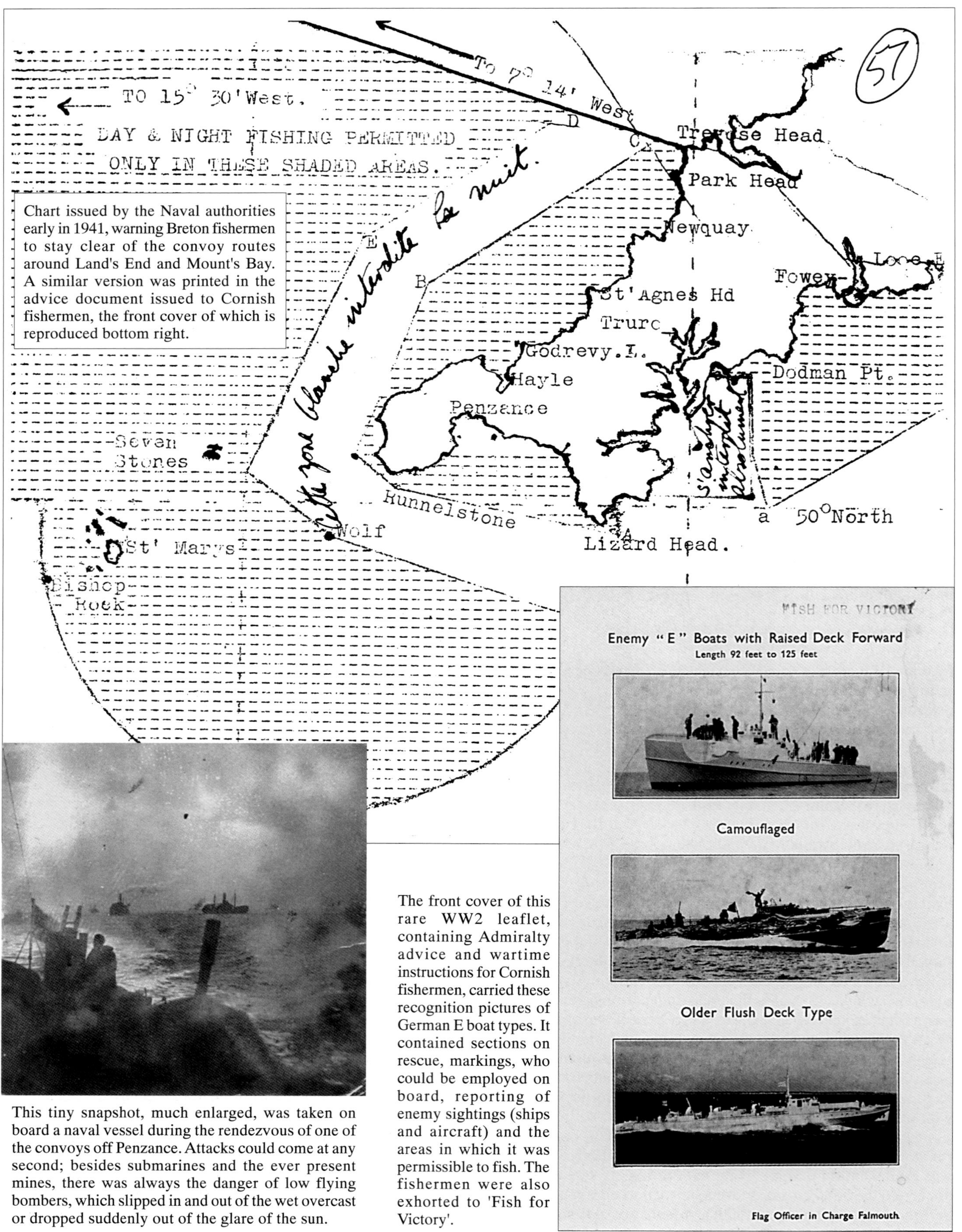

Chart issued by the Naval authorities early in 1941, warning Breton fishermen to stay clear of the convoy routes around Land's End and Mount's Bay. A similar version was printed in the advice document issued to Cornish fishermen, the front cover of which is reproduced bottom right.

This tiny snapshot, much enlarged, was taken on board a naval vessel during the rendezvous of one of the convoys off Penzance. Attacks could come at any second; besides submarines and the ever present mines, there was always the danger of low flying bombers, which slipped in and out of the wet overcast or dropped suddenly out of the glare of the sun.

The front cover of this rare WW2 leaflet, containing Admiralty advice and wartime instructions for Cornish fishermen, carried these recognition pictures of German E boat types. It contained sections on rescue, markings, who could be employed on board, reporting of enemy sightings (ships and aircraft) and the areas in which it was permissible to fish. The fishermen were also exhorted to 'Fish for Victory'.

floating away past the harbour and drifting ashore at Ponsandane where Naval bomb disposal teams found it was a German mine. The *Scillonian*, though fitted with degaussing gear against magnetic mines, operated largely from Newlyn, especially when shipping troops to garrison Scilly. She never steamed out into the bay but crept along close inshore, often inside Mousehole Island, at very slow speed for fear of detonating accoustic mines.

Sweeping these mines was always highly dangerous and, around noon one sunny Sunday morning, the trawler *Royalo*, a peacetime Grimsby fishing boat requisitioned at the start of the war, had just swept a string of magnetic mines laid close by the pierhead. The tide was very low and, as she turned seawards, the last mine in the row detonated with a roar that shook Penzance and left a dense coloumn of smoke. In minutes, only her masts and funnel top stood above the water but shore boats rescued nine survivors. So close in was the wreck that next morning the outward bound *Scillonian* had to edge around her to get to sea.

Equally dangerous were the fast and heavily armed flotillas of German destroyers which, after the fall of France, were based at Brest, only six hours steaming at 30 knots from their intended target, the convoy rendezvous point south of Mount's Bay. They were adept mine layers, slipping in very close to the Cornish coast and at Falmouth sank six ships in as many weeks, including the venerable old *Lady of the Isles*, which had sailed from Penzance for the last time that summer, having been requisitioned as a Naval cable ship. Only a few weeks later, ten of these destroyers came within two hours steaming of Scilly before being driven off by the cruisers *Newcastle* and *Emerald* in a running air and sea battle that ended only at the Ushant.

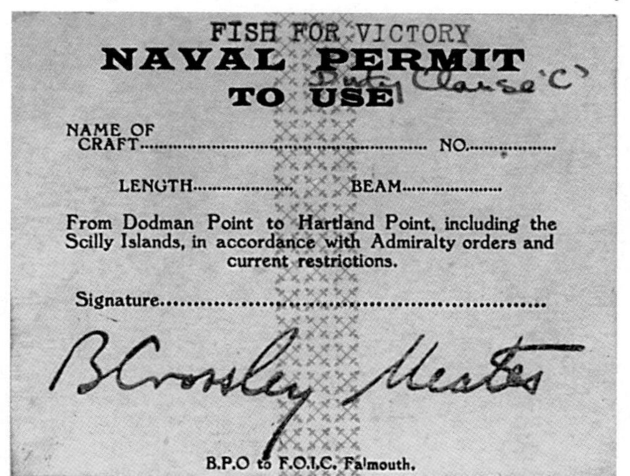
FISH FOR VICTORY

NAVAL PERMIT

TO USE

NAME OF CRAFT.. NO..................

LENGTH.................... BEAM....................

From Dodman Point to Hartland Point, including the Scilly Islands, in accordance with Admiralty orders and current restrictions.

Signature..

B.P.O to F.O.I.C. Falmouth.

There was another sortie on the evening of 24 November 1940, though a reconnaissance Junkers had already been shot down in the bay and its crew rescued by the Lizard lifeboat. Around midnight, the *Karl Galster*, *Hans Lody* and *Richard Beitzen* encountered a dozen darkened ships, not patrol boats but trawlers and drifters fishing out of Newlyn. The Belgian trawler *Simmone Marguerite* was sunk by gunfire, though her crew were rescued by another Belgian boat, the *Roger Denise*.

Then, at 3 a.m., German radar picked up a small convoy steaming across Mount's Bay from the Lizard. This had sailed at 17.30 from Plymouth and comprised the steamers *Stadion 11* and *Fernwood*, and the Dutch tanker *Appollonia*, which was in ballast for Avonmouth. Unlike her captain, the tanker's chief mate had been very reluctant to sail as the night was clear, calm and very dark, ideal weather for the German destroyers. His fears were realised when the *Appollonia* was suddenly illuminated by the searchlight of the *Karl Galster*, which immediately opened fire. Repeatedly hit on the bridge and upperworks, and with her funnel shot away, the *Appollonia* was abandoned just as her attacker fired two torpedoes into her. Twenty survivors got away in the boats but a Dutch engineer and thirteen coloured sailors were lost. The *Fernwood* escaped in the darkness and the *Stadion 11*, though heavily shelled, was left afloat when the Germans turned for home, belatedly pursued by British destroyers. Penlee lifeboat launched at 6am but found only 'a large patch of oil', though a fishing boat from Porthleven picked up a derelict barge, one of a pair slipped by the Falmouth tug *Lynch* when she almost ran into the sea battle.

The German destroyers eventually left Brest for the North Sea but the Luftwaffe remained in the skies above Mount's Bay, despite the arrival of Beaufighters and Hurricanes which, in the May of 1941, began operating from the newly opened airstrip at Pradannack, on the other side of the bay. Heavy night raids continued until, by the winter of 1942, 867 bombs had fallen on Penzance, most aimed at the harbour. Compared to the tremendous 'flak' put up by German occupied ports, the A-A defences at Penzance were slender, though the driver of a Mousehole bus remembers crouching in his cab during a night raid as shrapnel bounced off his roof!

Meanwhile, Land's End radio continued to pick up the familiar 'AAAA' (denoting aircraft attack), as on 8 March 1941, when the Norwegian steamer *Nurgis* was sunk and the Cardiff collier *Margo* was heavily damaged by dive bombers in the bay. Coxswain Frank Bluett, of Penlee lifeboat, recorded that he had taken onboard '*three injured men and one dead man, and the captain then asked that they be landed and bring out a doctor, as he had another bad case onboard*'. The wounded were tranferred to an ambulance on Penzance quay and a waiting doctor taken out to the *Margo*. Later, the lifeboat would be called to bring ashore another injured sailor from the steamer *Falvik*.

The whole rescue had been done in a hard NNE gale which prevented the lifeboat being re-housed but this was not the last rough wartime sortie. While searching for the dinghy of a crashed Halifax bomber in a wild southerly storm, the lifeboat was flung about so violently that the dry valve of the radio was jumped from its base; after a valiant struggle, it was replaced by the mechanic and coxswain Bluett sent a message to Land's End Radio asking that the Mousehole Life Saving Apparatus (LSA) Company use their search lights to guide him into Newlyn Harbour.

The bombers continued to strike at shipping in the bay, as on a fine summer's evening when a solitary Junkers came in at wavetop height and zooming over bombed an ancient concrete ship, which had served for years as a coal hulk. Occasionally, the bombers did not escape. Again a single Junkers hedge-hopped out of the dusk above Newlyn Harbour but, banking towards Mousehole, came within range of the *Capstone*, a big Hull trawler serving as patrol boat. The second round from the 12-pounder on her whaleback was a direct hit on the bomber's 'glasshouse'. Well ablaze but with its gunners still firing, the bomber lurched around Penlee Point and crashed behind Mousehole Island.

Many of the ships using Penzance were small Dutch coasters whose amiable and hardy crews were already familiar in Cornish ports, where many made their homes in the war years. Their English was often limited and caused hard-pressed shipping clerks to make errors; one coaster arrived to load at Hull instead of Goole, whilst the new cook for the *Evertzen*, of Delftzul, was shuttled around Cornwall for two weeks, only to find she was not the ship he wanted anyway. Spares and lubricants for their diesel engines were always a problem and scores of vital parts were machined in the Holman dry dock fitting shops, or by Bert Dyer, a first class engineer who had his own small workshop above Mousehole.

After an uneasy lull, war resumed in the bay when the Kreigsmarine struck at the flow of men and materials passing through western waters during the build up to D-Day. At 1.30 am. on 6 January 1944, the mechanic of Penlee lifeboat was alerted by Commander Walsh, the S.N.O. at Penzance, that a convoy had been attacked and '*several ships have been hit and some sunk, and their crews will . . . be on liferafts*'. He was also warned to '*make sure you turn on, before you launch, every light you've got, searchlight, navigation lights the lot . . . as this convoy has been attacked by E-boats and the naval craft won't take any chances*'. The night was clear as the *W. & S.* motored westwards at full speed in a freshening SW wind and then, guided by a dim red light, picked up two survivors, one with a broken leg. Another flare went up, revealing more survivors in the lifeboat's searchlights, '*the rafts being bright yellow . . . all you could see was faces. The water wasn't bad, so we got to the raft and shouted*' but sailors were so exhausted they had to be lifted bodily onboard the lifeboat and carried down to the cabin.

The Penlee lifeboat had rescued some of those who had survived one of the most disastrous convoy battles off west Cornwall. A few hours previously, a small convoy WP457, escorted by the destroyer *Mackay*, was southbound in the swept channel, butting into rough seas on the last of the ebb tide. Suddenly there was a roar of engines as seven German E-boats raced among the ships, not from seawards but looming out from the dark background of the land. Alerted by a reconnaissance Junkers, the E-boats, commanded by Leutenant-Commander Karl Muller, had slipped across from the Channel Islands at dusk and, mistaken for British MTBs, had lain in wait for the convoy between Porthcurno and the Runnelstone.

Their attack was devastating and the convoy broke in a wild melee, lit by tracer fire and starshells. The Naval escort trawler *Wallasea* was torpedoed and the London steamer *Underwood* blew up, scattering her deck cargo of lorries and invasion barges. The Norwegian steamer *Solstaad*, bound from Swansea to London with coal, left fourteen survivors to be picked up by Penlee lifeboat, while the *Polperro*, a Cornish owned Dutch coaster heavily loaded with coal from Manchester to Penryn, went down with all eight of her crew and three R.N.R. gunners. The dead and injured were landed back at Newlyn and once cleaned up, the Penlee lifeboat returned to the scene to search with the *Mackay* but their were no other survivors.

Ten days later, the E-boats struck another convoy but were driven away by the escorts and two of the Germans were badly damaged when they collided. They never returned again but the U-boats prowled around Mount's Bay until the last attack, on 21 March 1945. The little Dutch coaster *Pacific* was on the long run from Maryport to Penryn when she was torpedoed, close to the convoy RV. Penlee lifeboat made another of her long wartime sorties but the survivors were saved by the escorts. Her crew righted a capsized boat to see if anybody was underneath and then a frigate asked the coxswain to standby in case any of the German crew should come up, as the U-boat was already damaged and trapped on the bottom. The lifeboat hauled off and the 3rd Escort Group led by the frigate *Duckworth* resumed depth charging but there were no survivors from U-299. So the war ended in Mount's Bay, with the harbour unusually empty on V.E. Night, though *Satellite*, free of the wartime blackout, was lit overall.

V.E. Night in Penzance harbour. The *M.V. Satellite* was dressed with lights and sat shining brightly, visible from all round the bay, in silent tribute to those who were not coming back as much as in celebration of the end of hostilities.

The first warship to bear the name *Penzance* was a 6th rate of 24 guns, launched at Shoreham in April 1665. She spent most of her 18 year career patrolling or convoying ships on the Irish coast, seeing little action. The next *Penzance* was launched at Chichester in November 1747, taking part in the capture of Dominica in 1761 and the occupation of the French island of Martinique in January 1762. A few months later, she was in the fleet which supported the storming of Morro Castle, on the island of Havana. The third *H.M.S. Penzance* was a fleet escort sloop, launched at Devonport in April 1930. She saw wide service in the pre-war years and once, while on the Red Sea patrol, took as a passenger to Aden the Ethiopian Emperor Haile Selassie. She became a convoy escort at the break of war and was torpedoed on 24 August 1940, 700 miles west of Ireland. Her survivors were rescued by the steamer *Blairmore* but she was then herself sunk with tragic loss of life. Fifty eight years later, a magnificent new *H.M.S. Penzance*, a Sandown class minehunter, was commissioned in May 1998 and, following a visit to her namesake port in time for the Maritime Festival, will join the 3rd Mine Counter Measures Squadron, based at Faslane.

Chapter 6
Wrecks & Lifeboats

'The craft Richard Lewis *like a sea bird, now sighted, now hidden from view,*
Goes forth on her errand of mercy, to rescue the perishing crew;
'God speed her!' is murmured by thousands, as waves, like massed war horses prance,
And buoy up the beautiful lifeboat - the joy and pride of Penzance.'
Maritime Archive, Wreck of the Barque *North Britain* at Longrock, 6th December 1868

Another dramatic Victorian engraving, which depicts the launching of the Penzance lifeboat *Richard Lewis*, to the aid of the Glasgow barque *John Grey*, wrecked at Longrock in a SSW gale, while bound from Demerara to London on 6 January 1867.

Mount's Bay was always notorious for shipwrecks, when the Atlantic gales often drove sailing ships in to the surf swept sands between Penzance and St. Michael's Mount. One such disaster happened on an autumn night in 1760, when Penzance was roused by the ringing of alarm bells and the beating of drums. A great xebecca, the *Cavalla Bianca* (literally 'White Horse'), carrying eighteen 6-pounder guns and manned by Algerian corsairs and Turkish soldiers, had been wrecked on the Chimney Rock. By dawn, the vessel lay surrounded by '*men with long beards, standing in groups, with turbans on their heads and dead bodies lying on the sand*'. They were delighted to find that they had been wrecked in Cornwall and not on the coast of Spain, which was the target of their raid.

The wreck of the Spanish ship *Cavalla Bianca* in 1760.

Helped by a Penzance merchant, who having traded in the Levant could speak Italian and French, the corsair's crew were taken to the Barbican and fed by the townspeople. For fear of plague, they were then kept in quarantine for the next five weeks, until sent back to Algiers on a British warship.

There were many other wrecks and on 20 March 1812 a fisherman diarist recorded that '*This night seven vessels which were in the Mount Road riding, parted and was driven on shore. Three to the Westward . . . are an entire wreack . . out of which four or five men and a boy was drownded.*'

Stranded ships were often looted by coast dwellers and tin miners who descended from the bleak moors. If the ship's cargo was tobacco, brandy or rum, a drunken riot was inevitable, although

The *Jeunne Hortense*, stranded at Long Rock in May 1888 and this photograph shows her struggling close in whilst the lifeboat *Richard Lewis* is being prepared for launching. There was an element of black humour with this incident, as there was a dead body in a coffin on board the brigantine, which led to a few comments along the lines of '*dawn worree about ee, ee cun flawt ashore isself!*' The *Jeunne Hortense* was towed back to the dry dock where, beyond economic repair, she was broken up for firewood. Two other vessels also suffered strandings in this storm; the *Otto*, subsequently bought by Denleys and renamed *Providence* and the *Nulli Secundus*, a German brigantine originally named *Tobacco,* which had previously stranded on the Eastern Green in 1865.

The Liverpool square-rigger *Cromdale* had, at one stage in his sailing career, provided a berth for the painter John Joseph Urens. On 23 May 1915, she was 124 days out from Chile, bound for Falmouth with a cargo of nitrates and already a week overdue, when she ran into dense fog as she neared the Lizard. She grounded on the rocks below Bass Point and, badly holed, settled rapidly by the stern, having to be abandoned with ten minutes. Next morning, in clear weather, she presented an awesome spectatcle, with every sail set but hanging limply from the yards in the still air and the crew managed to get back on board to salvage some belongings and the ship's instruments. The wreck was subsequently auctioned for the paltry sum of £41 but with a ruined cargo it was really only her sailing gear that had any value. She broke up in a heavy SSW gale a week later and little salvage was ever carried out on the remains.

The old collier brigantine *Henry Harvey*, unable to get home with her cargo of coal in a hard NE gale, came round to shelter off Penzance but was driven onto the Battery Rocks. The lifeboat landed her crew and the brigantine survived the wreck but was eventually 'posted' whilst bound for France some years later.

sometimes the authorities managed to arrive in time. In April 1818 when the wine-laden Swedish brig *Victoria* was blown ashore, the country people swarmed on board but were promptly driven away by the Penrith Yeomanry, who came galloping over the sands waving their sabres.

Penzance had one of the first lifeboats in Cornwall, becoming a regular R.N.L.I. station in 1856. Sailors, pilots and coastguards donned the cork jacket and woollen cap to row lifeboats like the *Richard Lewis* and the *Elizabeth & Blanche* into the heroic pages of R.N.L.I. history. On a stormy January evening in 1867, the *Richard Lewis* was launched into the surf opposite St. Michael's Mount and rescued the crews of two imperilled schooners; 48 hours later, it was out in the same wicked seas and saved thirteen sailors from the Glasgow-registered Westindiaman *John Grey*, wrecked towards midnight during a tremendous SSW gale.

There was even greater heriosm and drama after a Prussia Cove coastguard sighted a barque coming westwards into the bay, half hidden by mist and driving rain. The coastguards followed her with their rocket waggon, along the narrow clifftop lanes. They were impressed by the way the barque was being handled among the reefs and shoaling water. The vessel had also been sighted from Penzance, with the pilot gig *May Girl* putting out from the harbour and if the barque had held her course there was a chance that she could have been run onto the sands by the lighthouse pier. As the gig cleared the 'Gaps', however, the barque ceased her westerly track and, instantly becoming embayed close to Longrock, let go both anchors. The pilots were close enough to see her part her chains and strike, close to the reef. Just then, three enormous seas broke over the gig and the pilots put down the helm for home, though not before they were able to make out on the barque's counter her name, *North Britain*.

Launched at Picton, Nova Scotia, in 1838, the *North*

The Liverpool coaster *Primrose* rammed her bows onto Low Lee Ledge in thick fog on 3 August 1906. She was captured by a local postcard photographer the following morning, by which time her stern had risen twenty feet in the air. She sank in deep water shortly after.

Baltic wrecked. Nov: 1st 1907

On the night of 1 November 1907, when the weather was thick and rough, the Thames sailing barge *Baltic* was inward bound for Newlyn, with cement for the new harbour works, when she ran onto Mousehole Island. Her crew were saved by Mousehole fishermen but the non appearance of the Penzance lifeboat, which stuck in the harbour mud, led to rancour and some unflattering doggerel verse. Contrary to popular belief, the *Baltic* was filled with barrels and refloated, ending her days as a hulk in an Essex creek.

One of the many 'Yorkies', or east coast steam drifters, that sailed from Penzance during the mackerel season, the *Renown* of Yarmouth, ran ashore behind the Albert Pier on 3 February 1909. She was only saved by the quick thinking of the lifeboat crew, who took a hawser from her to a capstan on the pierhead. The lifeboat is the *Cape of Good Hope*, which had come down from Yorkshire a year previously to replace the *Elizabeth & Blanche.*

Britain was an old softwood 'Bluenose' barque, and had sailed from Quebec at 9 a.m. on 4 November 1868, loaded with 950 stands of timber, prime deals and baulks for Southampton. She was commanded by Captain John Rogers, a veteran seaman who had never been wrecked in thirty two years at sea. He and eight men tried to come through the surf in the jolly boat but she capsized and among the rescuers who waded out chest deep was William Jeffrey, the champion Cornish wrestler. Meanwhile, hundreds of spectators watched the drama unfold, many of whom had come out on the early afternoon train or by horse bus.

The *Richard Lewis* launched into the surf but an hour had elasped before Coxswain Carbis could get alongside the poop, where those left onboard crouched for shelter. Instantly, the lifeboat was struck squarely on her bow by a big sea and capsized; her crew, some under the boat, others swimming for dear life, managed to get back aboard, though Ned Hodge, one of two lifeboatman brothers, drifted ashore and was rescued by a local coalman who rode his horse into the waves. Battered, bruised and exhausted, the lifeboatmen ran the *Richard Lewis* back onto the beach, where a call for volunteers instantly procured a fresh crew and, conned by the valiant Chief Officer Blackmore of the coastguard, she again put off.

Dusk was falling before the lifeboat ranged alongside the *North Britain* and the volunteers were thrown about so violently that Anthony Pascoe, the coastguard who first sighted the barque, broke three ribs. Eight sailors were taken off and landed, amid the rousing cheers of the onlookers and even as the *North Britain* began going to pieces in the surf. The rescue led to the awarding of no less than five R.N.L.I. Silver Medals; among the recipients was Samuel Higgs, a young mining engineer and businessman, whose medal can be seen at the Penlee House museum.

Rescues like that of the *North Britain* would be recorded on the lifeboat service boards right up to the last days of sail in Mount's Bay. The Norwegian brig *Otto* was 58 days out from Bahia to Falmouth when she was wrecked in a '*heavy rolling sea*', in January 1873. Lit by patent 'Phospherescent Lamps', the *Richard Lewis*, at the third attempt, rescued eight men, a dog and a pig! Five nights later, an easterly hurricane had already wrecked the schooners *Rose* and *Treaty* off the Albert Pier when the lifeboat, held in shelter of the railway station, was called to the Eastern Green. Peering into the icy blast of rain, spray and sand, the lifeboatmen could just make out the schooner *Marie Emilie*, of Lorient, homeward bound with coal from Cardiff. Twice the lifeboat was tossed onto the schooner's decks and twice driven away but although with four oars broken, she saved all on board.

In 1885, the veteran *Richard Lewis* was replaced by the *Dora* and a handsome new lifeboat house, complete with bell tower for calling her crew, was built on Wharf Road. There were many more heroic rescues but call outs grew less as sail declined in the bay. Getting the lifeboat carriage across the harbour mud at low tide was always a serious disadvantage and finally, in 1908, the *Elizabeth & Blanche*, which had replaced the *Dora*, was transferred to Newlyn. She was replaced by the *Cape of Good Hope*, a slightly smaller self-righting lifeboat, transferred from Runswick Bay in Yorkshire.

One wreck embedded in local legend is that of the Newlyn lugger *Diana* whose crew, after a hard night's fishing off the Lizard, turned in, leaving one fisherman on watch who unfortunately went below to light his pipe and fell asleep. Luckily the '*boat knawed 'er way ome*' and at daylight, on 5 July 1905, early morning bathers were astonished to find her high and dry on the Hamburgans Rocks, off the Promenade. Shouts and thumps on the hull brought the sleepy fishermen on deck but the lugger stayed ashore under public gaze until the late afternoon tide. Her crew's embarrasment must have been doubled by a ribald song, sung to an old revival hymn:–

'*Steer for the Prom Boys, Steer for the Prom,*
Never mind the rocks boys, steer for the Prom.
Safe in the old Diana*, cleave to your self no more,*
So never mind the rocks boys and steer for the shore.'

Other wrecks had their light hearted or even funny side, like the salvors who were lugging a 'salvaged' liferaft up a cliff when it suddenly inflated, or the chain of helpers who obligingly passed stores and gear up the cliff, where it then 'disappeared' into the countryside. There was another intrepid 'wrecker' who, when burying his loot, a very large brass porthole, in a secluded gulley, returned later only to find it buried under a cliff fall. There were also the salvors who were busily shovelling shingle out of a stranded yacht when they suddenly realised most of her side had gone and they were digging up the beach!

The 32-foot self righter *Elizabeth & Blanche* being launched from the Abbey Slip around the turn of the century. It was this laborious manoeuvre which ultimately led to the close of the lifeboat station at Penzance.

Only six days before the Armistice in November 1918, the Yankee steamer *Lake Harris* dragged ashore on Longrock beach during a southerly gale. Resplendent in dazzle paint and with 12-pounder gun pointing towards the Mount, she drew scores of sightseers despite the efforts of coastguards and naval sentries.

The Navy sent down two rescue tugs, the *Epic* and the *Blazer*, but they had chosen a bad night to get her off. The lookout of the salvage steamer, the *Lady of the Isles*, which was anchored close by, was astonished to see the two tugs at times '*pulling in opposite directions'*. The *Lake Harris* suddenly came off with a rush and the *Epic*, in trying to get between her and the shore, ran squarely onto the Rymon Rocks.

The American coaster *Lake Harris,* stranded on Longrock beach in November 1918, shows off her anti U-boat, dazzle paint.

She fired distress rockets but neither the *Lady* nor the *Blazer* dared come alongside. However, the *Lady*'s searchlight soon picked out the Penlee lifeboat *Elizabeth & Blanche* rowing round to the tug. The wartime call-up of sailors and fishermen meant that she was manned by a scratch crew and consequently, on the rowing benches sat a couple of policemen, some of the regular crew, and soldiers, bluejackets and a young merchant sailor, all on leave.

Fifty years later the young sailor recalled that memorable night; '*God knows how we got down there and God knows how we got back, with every other man looking over his shoulder to see where we were going!*' The *Epic* was later refloated by the *Lady of the Isles* but the *Blazer* subsequently went over to Scilly and got herself wrecked on St. Mary's.

An R.N.L.I. Silver Medal was earned in sight of Penzance Promenade in one of the most daring rescues in the bay. The Cornish steam collier *Taycraig* left Plymouth, to load roadstone at Newlyn, on a Sunday evening in Janaury 1936 and '*rounded the Lizard in the early hours of the following morning . . . there was a strong to gale force SW wind*'. The young A.B. on watch was '*happy at the thought of getting into calmer waters*'. He was to be disappointed as the storm increased and though the collier was sounding her whistle, the pilot boat could not leave Newlyn. Suddenly she was swept

A sketch showing the Naval tug *Epic* impaled on Rymon Rocks.

The wreck of the *Taycraig*, 27 January 1936.

by a *'very heavy rain squall which caused the wind to back SE and increase to severe gale'*. Mate William Billing, an old schoonerman, was driven off the fo'c'stle head back to the lower bridge and Captain Moss dropped anchor but the *Taycraig* struck the Gear Rocks, level with the tall navigational beacon.

The young A.B. ran to rouse a fireman in the fo'c'stle and they ran aft to help launch the boats but '*were driven off by heavy seas*'. Captain Moss kept sounding S.O.S. on the siren, while they fired rockets and flares, and also set light to bedding soaked in parafin – so successfully that onshore they thought the collier was on fire. The *Taycraig* was fast sinking by the stern and the crew made their way to the fo'c'stle head, the rest of the vessel being submerged and pounded by heavy seas. The suddenly appearing lights of the lifeboat were a very welcome sight to the crew. Coxswain Bluett played his searchlight on the *Taycraig* and though the lifeboat's port engine had failed, grappelled the collier's bows, and Captain Moss and his eight crew were saved. Three days later the collier broke up and sank on the Gear Rocks. Though much of her was salvaged, enough was left to be colonised by marine plants and creatures, and is today studied as a sea life centre.

Wrecks still happen despite all the modern navigational aids, though seldom with such desperate outcomes as in sailing ship days. The author recalls seeing a small salvage ship leave Penzance and, mistaking all previous directions, carefully steam the wrong side of every buoy and daymark! Similarly, the Belgian trawler *Normauwil* ran ashore on the Cressars Rock on 8 February 1988 in a fresh south west gale, after steering the wrong side of the pole. The pilot boat and the jetboat *Sundancer* came to her aid but she was refloated by the Penlee lifeboat.

In 1912, the *Janet Hoyle*, the last true Penzance lifeboat had arrived on station, having been personally selected by Coxswain Nicholls at the R.N.L.I. depot at Poplar, after service at Ayr in Scotland. Her most arduous service came in the Boxing Day Hurricane of 1912, when launched in mountainous seas to search for the Italian steamer *Tripolitania*. She got home with the bow planks split off the stem post and great patches scoured in her paint work.

Eventually, in 1916, because of the launching problems at Penzance, the lifeboat station was closed and the boat transferred to Newlyn. The old 1885-built lifeboat house still stands, however, as a reminder of those days. Nowadays, it is the local R.N.L.I. branch gift and souvenir shop, and houses an exhibition dedicated to the history of the Penzance and Penlee lifeboat stations.

Penzance harbour remains a hazardous landfall in a hard southerly gale, as the French trawler *Viergal* discovered around dawn on 13 December 1973. Running for shelter after developing engine trouble, she failed to round the Lighthouse Pier and drove into the surf off the railway station. The trawlermen owed their lives to the bravery of the crew of a Whirlwind helicopter from R.N.A.S. Culdrose.

An engraving of the lifeboat race on 10 September 1867, held in celebration of the new timber-built lifeboat house on the promenade at Penzance. Six boats took part; the *Richard Lewis* of Penzance, the *Moses* of St. Ives, the *Cousins Wm. & Mary Ann of Bideford* of Sennen, the *Isis* of Hayle, the *Agar Robartes* of Porthleven and the *Daniel J. Draper* of Mullion. After a hard rowed race, the Sennen boat won, with Penzance coming second and the Hayle boat third.

Chapter 7
Divers & Salvors

'Dec 9th. . . received an application from the Cornish Salvage Co. per Mr. Chenalls, for permission to bring the Russian Barque Ymer *to the harbour to be broken up.'* Penzance Dock Report Book 1912.

One of the *Greencastle*'s divers descends to inspect the bows of the Cardiff collier *River Ely*, which was towed into dock after grounding on Mousehole Island in August 1924.

Where ever there are shipwrecks, there will always be salvors and Penzance, lying amid one of the most dangerous stretches of the Cornish coast, has traditionally been the home port for generations of divers and salvage men. Whether a ship was on the rocks, or sunk to her mast tops, they would methodically strip her of machinery and cargo. In slack times they would steam off to a long-forgotten wreck in one of the more inaccessible coves or, perhaps alerted by a friendly fisherman, drop a diver onto some lonely reef or shoal in search of cannons or gold dollars.

Working this underwater harvest was a flotilla of small salvage ships, including such as the *Greencastle*, an ex-North Sea trawler turned wrecking boat. For twenty years she was manned by a tough brotherhood of divers and salvors, who sailed under the flag of the legendary Western Marine Salvage Company. The 'Greeny', as she was popularly known, even managed to leave a souvenir of her wrecking days, a bronze cannon – in fact a French demi culverin of around 1640 – raised by her whilst working the wreck of the collier *Primrose* on Low Lee Ledge in 1916. Today, this cannon can be seen outside the Penzance Public Library (*as pictured on page 7*).

One particular story from Cornish salving folklore encapsulates the tough brotherhood tradition. There were two

This uncompromising bunch, posing nonchalently for the camera in about 1905, are the crew of the salvage vessel *Greencastle*. It was a hard life and these were tough men but always ready to help a ship in distress.

In April 1903, the *Greencastle* went over to Loe Bar, near Porthleven, where Captain Henry Anderson, diver and shipsalvor supreme, raised a large iron cannon from the wreck of the frigate *Anson*, which went down in December 1807. The top view shows Captain Anderson about to descend. Later, the salvors with their ladyfolk and children, posed with the gun in the Artillery Rooms at Penzance.

divers who regularly worked off the 'Greeny' and legend has it that one hot day, whilst working the wreck of the battleship *Montague* on Lundy, they got into a violent argument over one supposedly 'purloining' pieces of scrap from the other's pile. Resorting to blows, they proceeded to beat each other insensible, collapsing on the 'Monty's' deck. On recovering, they shook hands and were the best of friends from that day on.

Following her grounding at Lamorna in 1904, the *Lady of the Isles* was refloated a few days later by the Little Western Salvage Company, who subsequently bought her and, for another thirty years following her mishap, she served distressed ships all over the south west approaches. In between incidents at sea, diving and scrapping operations carried on as normal but such work was always suspended to help a distressed ship, such as in January 1920 when the *Lady of the Isles* crossed the bay to rescue the French steam trawler *Anenome*, ashore at Porthleven.

The *Lady* and the *Greencastle* could often be seen working together, to rescue distressed or disabled ships, as they did when bringing in the Greek steamer *Jannikis* in November 1921. Travelling in ballast from Rouen to Fowey, the *Jannikis* had been blown ashore on Praa Sands but, working in tandem, the two Little Western Salvage vessels managed to tow her off and then brought her into Penzance together.

Sometimes the trip to a ship in trouble brought scant reward although it was never in vain. In March 1920, during a dense fog, several vessels ran ashore on the Cornish coast, including the Lowestoft steam drifter *Golden Gift*, which was heading in with her catch when she ran onto the Larrigan Rocks, off the Promenade. The salvage vessels came out but she ebbed dry and warped off on the flood tide. The salvors attendance was still important, in case unrealised damage had been caused, or if the vessel got into further difficulties when manoeuvering free.

One notable salvage failure was the Italian steamer *Tripolitania*, of Genoa. She was in ballast for Cardiff on Boxing Day 1912 when she was driven onto Loe Bar by an easterly hurricane. There ensued a year of unremitting salvage work; shovel gangs, towage and hydraulic jacks were all tried and eventually they got her to the water's edge, at which point another SW gale blew up and drove the *Tripolitania* back up the beach. Dispirited, the salvors gave up and the steamer was sold for scrap.

There were plenty of wrecks from the First World War along the coast and so, in between other work, the salvage boats at Penzance could always be kept busy piling the quays high with machinery, propellors and steel plate from this ready source. Between the wars also, the *Lady* often deputised for the *R.M.S. Scillonian* too, back on the service where she began her career, or was hired for undersea telegraph cable work. These trips could be very rough, as confirmed

The *Anenome* ashore, with the *Lady of the Isles* in attendance.

The terrifying reality of a wreck; the Italian steamer *Tripolitania*, on Loe Bar, 26 December 1912. In the view below, the salvage gang attempt to dig her clear of the sand in what, after a year of work, was ultimately to prove a futile attempt to save the vessel.

Having been refloated following her mishap at Lamorna in September 1904 – with the aid of Holman's yard who made some bolt-on plates to cover the damage – *Lady of the Isles* was carefully brought back to Penzance by the *Greencastle*, leading, and another salvage tug the *Saxon*, from Falmouth.

The Fleetwood trawler *Maud* broke tow off the Lizard, whilst bound for the Isle of Man on 11 February 1912, drifting ashore at Kynance Cove. Just four days later, the big French bounty clipper *Chilli*, bound to Falmouth for orders from Iquiquie with nitrates, almost joined the *Maud* in fresh and foggy weather but was hauled clear by a Falmouth tug. With the mist having lifted, the view **above right** shows the tug hauling her away, whilst the *Maud* still wallows in the surf. The 1920s snapshot, **left**, shows bathers at Kynance posing in front of the remains of the trawler's engine and boiler, valuable scrap which, most unusually, was not quickly scooped up by the salvors.

The Greek steamer *Jannikis* is towed into Penzance by the *Lady of the Isles*, after stranding on Praa Sands in November 1921. Close in, the *Lady*'s salvage mate *Greencastle* fusses around behind the steamer, helping, with the aid of another hawser, to keep her on course.

'A fighter till the end' The Death of H.M.S. Warspite

The story of the redundant battleship *Warspite* is probably the most incredible saga in the history of Cornish rescue and salvage. Whilst on her way to a shipbreakers on the Clyde in 1948, the *Warspite* parted company from the tugs towing her in a south westerly gale and was quickly driven right into Mount's Bay. Despite huge seas, the running crew of seven were saved by the Penlee lifeboat *W. & S.*, coxswain Edwin Madron. Once the gales had abated, the old battleship still constituted 30,000 tons of assorted scrap but now firmly wedged on the rocks of Prussia Cove.

There were several bids to refloat her and resume the journey to Scotland but she was still there when a sister battleship, *Anson*, steamed into Mount's Bay on a courtesy visit in the summer of 1949. A year later, the press, the BBC and a large crowd gathered expectantly as the battle ship, buoyed up by twenty-four air compressors filling her compartments, bumped afloat. Unfortunately, there was insufficient water to clear the reefs and a rising SW gale forced the salvors to retreat into the Bay. The elderly ex-trawler *Barnet*, which was the workhorse of the salvage operations, spent the night moored up under the battleship's bows but

was holed in the engine room. After her crew were taken off by the Admiralty tug *Freebooter*, the *Barnet* drifted ashore off Longrock, the first of many mishaps.

The *Warspite* was finally beached off St. Michael's Mount in August 1950 and, having been considerably lightened, there was another bid to refloat her hulk that November. The Falmouth tug *Masterman* tried to tow her to a survey position off the Mount but ran ashore and spent the night on the Hogus Rocks. The tug *Tradesman* tried to tow her sister clear next morning but got sixty foot of steel wire around her propellor, wedged so tight that it took a diver a day to free her. Penlee lifeboat stood by as the *Barnet* towed the *Tradesman* to Newlyn but, in the stormy blackness, the tug almost drifted ashore before being warped into the harbour.

The *Barnet*, which was forever breaking down or breaking loose, much to the irritation of the Penzance Harbour Master, was one of a small flotilla of scrap boats which was employed on the salvage. The *Radnore* was an ex-landing craft, launched at Warren Point in 1944 and was usually towed to the job by the *Barnet*. Once in position she was loaded with scrap steel by the two large cranes which had been erected on the battleship's bridge section, after she had been cut in half to aid the work. Once alongside the Albert Pier the steel was loaded into railway wagons with the aid of an ancient shunting crane, along a spur from the station which, having been taken up sometime before the war, was relaid in July 1948. Some of the steel scrap also went by sea and among the vessels taking the old *Warspite* away in bits was the auxiliary schooner *Result*, which sailed from the Albert Pier for Newport on 12 July 1952.

Another tug employed was the *Chew Magna*, notorious for her attempt to tow the newly completed (by Holman's) King Harry Ferry from Penzance to Falmouth in January 1951, which ended with the vessel breaking loose and narrowly avoiding being wrecked on the Lizard. In 1953, the fleet was joined by the old Severn trow *Emperor*, which motored down from Bristol and spent the next few years as a scrap barge, before eventually being dumped and burned on the beach at Ponsandane, where her keelson still appears at low tide.

In August 1954, the *Warspite* was moved 130 feet closer inshore, aided by her compressors and two jet engines from an experimental aircraft. The marathon salvage job cost two lives and was never fully finished as, though the old warship had finally disappeared from view by the summer of 1955, fragments of her boilers and chains still lie in the shallows of the Mount. The full story of this heroic episode in maritime history is only now being written and will provide a fitting epitaph for one of the Royal Navy's most famous battleships.

The pictures show, **opposite top:** the Penlee lifeboat battling in running seas to get the skeleton crew of seven off the *Warspite*, shortly after she had broken her tow; **opposite bottom:** the partially scrapped hulk with the salvage tugs *Englishman* and *Tradesman* alongside; **this page top:** the Warspite's hulk after it had been cut in two amidships, with the salvage cranes working onboard and St. Michael's Mount in the background; **this page above:** a close up of one of the midships sections, with scrapping nearing completion as the two cranes work backwards towards each other.

The salvage vessel *Crazy Diamond* sits on the sand at Tresco whilst she lands cargo, a task for which her flat bottom is ideally suited. Her 'Puffer' origins are still evident, despite much modification over the years for her new role. Owner Captain Steve Palk named her after the Pink Floyd song 'Shine on you Crazy Diamond' and it does appear rather apt. The second view below shows her on salvage work at sea.

by entries in her log while outward bound for Valencia Island, County Kerry, under charter to Western Union Telegraph in the autumn of 1928.

With the outbreak of the Second World War in 1939, the *Lady of the Isles* was requisitioned by the Admiralty, who sent her to Falmouth to be refitted as a cable ship for service at Capetown. On 2 October 1940, the *Lady* was outward bound for Southampton behind the tug *Aid* when they were both sunk by German mines.

One remarkable new addition to the great tradition of sea salvage vessels at Penzance was the *Crazy Diamond*, an ex-Admiralty 'Puffer', originally the *V.I.C. 35*, which was launched at Liverpool in 1945. In October 1975, she was bought by Captain Stephen Palk of Penzance, who converted her into a remarkable small salvage ship. Her steam engine went to an industrial museum, being replaced by a Paxman diesel made surplus during work on the old 'Highlands & Islands' vessel *Norwest Laird* at Hayle. The *Crazy Diamond*'s first mast and navigation lights came from the minesweeper *Warsash*, under demolition at Hayle; some years later, it was replaced by a section of trawling gantry rescued from the wrecked trawler *Conqueror*, which also provided a searchlight and other gear.

Like her predecessors, the *Crazy Diamond* became a 'maid of all work', handling heavy lifts like the harbour gates and often running cargo to the Scilly Isles, where her flat bottom meant she could beach out on Tresco or St. Martins, as well as working wrecks. Occasionally, she ventured further, recovering anchors for supertankers in Torbay and in 1981, salvaging the coaster *St. Bedan*, which had been blown up by the IRA while inward bound to Moville near Derry. Her odd name came from a record by the rock group Pink Floyd and aptly reflects the eccentricity which has always been endemic in the world of marine salvage.

The Belgian trawler *Normauwil* being towed in after going ashore on the Cressars Rock in February 1988. There will always be work for the salvors around the coast of west Cornwall.

Almost fifty years after her rescue of the skeleton crew of the *Warspite*, the ex-Penlee lifeboat *W. & S.*, now renamed and refitted as the handsome motor yacht *Atlantic* of Belfast, returned to the scene of her previous exploits and has since become a regular visitor to the harbour.

Chapter 8
Lights, Tenders and Lighthouses

May 2nd. The Elder Brethren of Trinty House have sanctioned the altering of the Pier-head light from double flash every 30 seconds to double flash every 15 seconds. This can be effected with very little expense and will make the light more distinctive from seaward. Penzance Dock Report Book 1914.

More Victorian drama, although this time, given that conditions around the Wolf Rock at times would be difficult to exaggerate anyway, it is probably fairly close to the reality. This engraving shows the keepers being landed on the rock following completion of the lighthouse in 1871. This was one of the first lighthouses designed with toilets for the keepers and the stepped base, shown as rings on the engraving, had the effect of preventing waves from sweeping up the tower. The vessel is the Trinity House paddle tug *Wolf.*

A pinnacle of porphory jutting into the deep Atlantic, the lonely Wolf, or 'Gulph' as it was called by Elizabethan mariners, was first marked by a beacon in 1793 – a tall mast '*leaded into the rock with six iron stays'*. It was soon swept away and forty years elapsed before another mast, of foot square English oak, crowned the rocks in 1840, though such was the weather that only thirty working days of ten hours each had been possible over the five years. The mast vanished the following winter, as did a larger iron replacement sometime later but the conical base of the fourth remains beside the modern light.

The Corporation of Trinity House established a depot at Penzance when, in October 1861, they embarked upon the immense task of building a lighthouse on the Wolf Rock. James Walker, the celebrated lighthouse engineer, proposed a new tower, 116 feet high and using 2,397 tons of Cornish granite, something far more substantial than the beacons which had previously been erected and quickly swept away. Building a lighthouse on such rock, exposed to the open Atlantic, was a large, labourious and very long operation and Penzance was a natural base for Trinity House to keep their construction fleet. Accordingly, they leased a small yard next to the Customs house.

This more recent comparison view shows the launch of the Trinity House vessel *Satellite*, laying off the Wolf Rock in very rough weather. The lighthouse now has a helicopter platform atop it, the construction of which was itself no mean feat.

A view from the end of the South Pier in 1880. Work on rebuilding and extending the harbour is underway. The steamer in the foreground is the old Trinity House tender *Mermaid*. Behind its funnel, construction of the new quay wall has closed the old entrance to the dry dock, whilst further to the right, a steam crane is laying granite blocks to form the north arm of what, in 1884, became the new wet dock. Behind the *Mermaid*'s masts can be seen the lofts, stores and offices of the Mathews family, who also owned the dry dock. To their left is the Custom House and the Trinity House depot, and also a slipway, soon to be buried behind the new quay wall.

Two views showing the original, **top**, and later, **bottom**, Longships Lighthouses off Land's End, also serviced by the Trinity tenders from the depot at Penzance. Lieut. Henry Smith, who attempted the first beacon on the Wolf Rock, was also involved with the first Longships Lighthouse of 1795, although it was soon taken over by Trinity House. The replacement was completed in 1873 and, as can be seen from the photographs, the rock itself was substantially reprofiled as well. It survives today, now fully automated – as are all the British lighthouses – and complete with helicopter platform on top.

An unusual view of the Lighthouse Pier, Penzance, in the 1890s. The lighthouse, which is still in use today, was built in 1853 of iron rings cast at the Copperhouse Foundry at Hayle. The vessel coming into harbour is the schooner *Mary James*.

A 1950s view of the *THV Satellite* in the wet dock at Penzance.

Launched in 1924 by Thornycroft of Southampton, the 507 ton Trinity tender *Satellite* spent most of her career sailing out of Penzance, with many local sailors numbered amongst her crew. Many tales are still jokingly told of her and of the distinctive pigtail of smoke always dragging in her wake. Indeed, a lifeboat was once launched to her when a passing vessel reported that the old tender was on fire. After thirty years of hard service, she finally left Penzance in the spring of 1963 and was sold soon after to Belgian shipbreakers.

Here, masons dressed the blocks of granite, which were hauled in by heavy waggons from the quarries at Lamorna Cove, before being loaded onto trolleys and pushed along a small tramroad that ran across the quayside and onto a wooden jetty. They were then craned onto barges, which were towed out to the Wolf Rock by the aptly-named Trinity paddle tug *Wolf*. The laborious process of unloading the blocks and hoisting them up onto the new works by means of a derrick was then carried out. This was also a dangerous process and all hands had to wear lifejackets all of the time, something which may seem obvious to us today but actually quite an unusual requirement in that pre-'Health and Safety' age.

Even after the Wolf Rock Light began flashing on New Year's Eve 1871, Trinity House kept their depot and offices at Penzance. Trinity tenders like the *Mermaid* and the *Siren*, resplendent in their black and

Trinity House workers photographed loading a buoy onboard the tender *Satellite* sometime in the 1950s.

A 1930s holiday snapshot which also happens to show the gear pole beacon, off Penzance. The ball-shaped cage acted as a daymark, warning vessels to keep clear of the rocks here.

The Lighthouse Pier on a stormy day around 1880. The photograph is doubly interesting in that it also shows the signalling mast, on the left, used to indicate to ships in the bay whether or not the harbour gates were open. If conditions were rough, a ball was hoisted to show the gates were closed, as seen here.

cream livery, became frequent visitors to the port, on their trips to service buoys, or when calling at the local lighthouses. There were many other lighthouses and beacons whch needed serving by the Trinity tenders, all around the west Cornish coast, as well as the Seven Stones Lightship.

The rapid modernisation of Trinity House, which began in the early 1980s, brought many changes to the service. Appropriately, the automation of the lightships began at Penzance with the drydocking of *LV 93* by N. Holman & Sons in September 1980. The task involved the complete stripping out of the vessel and the installation of complex electrical and electronic equipment; even the traditional name of the station, painted along the LV's side, was replaced by boards mounted on the superstructure for ease of maintainence.

LV93 was undocked in December of that year, becoming the brand new Channel Lightvessel. She was followed by the old Scarweather Lightvessel, the first of a further ten that were to be automated by Holmans. The author began his career as a 'ship's sign writer' on these lightvessels and still ruefully recalls the day when the Trinity 'super' reprimanded him for having pink instead of white letters. Puzzled, as when last seen the lettering was pristine white, he realised that the paint sprayers had been working with red paint and in a breeze the night before.

With the automation of the lightships, which included even the Seven Stones vessel, and then the rock lighthouses, which sprouted helicopter platforms atop their lanterns, there was less need of a fleet of tenders. As a consequence, the *Stella* was the last to call, and that only a courtesey visit, in August 1985. Trinity House still keeps a depot at Penzance, while the adjacent Buoy Hall has become the National Lighthouse Centre, which houses a magnificent collection of equipment and machinery. Pendeen Lighthouse, guardian of the biggest steamship graveyard in Cornwall, is now also fully automated but it too is open to visitors.

Chapter 9
The Dry Dock

'Particulars, Plan, Photographs and Conditions of Sale of FREEHOLD PROPERTY comprising A DRY DOCK, Coal Yard and Sheds, Cottages, Plots and other Premises Which will be Sold by Auction IN ONE LOT'. Auction Poster 25 August 1904.

For over a century now, spectators have gathered to watch ships enter or leave the dry dock. In this view, people crowd the Ross Bridge as the 827 ton iron barque *Moltke*, of Hamburg, warps herself into the Abbey turning basin in April 1886, only a couple of years after the new dry dock had opened. She had just discharged grain from Koenigsburg, for Branwell's Mills and, after a spell in dry dock, when Captain Krauz opened his vessel up to the public, she took on 300 tons of roadstone ballast and sailed for Cardiff to load with coal for home. Following the harbour improvements of the 1880s, a new entrance had to be provided for Mathew's dry dock, which was realigned, enlarged and given new gates, although, from work carried out on them over ninety years later, it seems that the old gates may just have been rehung. The new gates opened into the Abbey turning basin, in turn accessed from the main harbour via the iron swing bridge seen.

The Holman expertise in steam engineering meant that their fitters and smiths were much in demand by the screw steamers and paddle packets which, by the 1850s, were calling regularly at Penzance. Old ledgers are filled with requests to repair leaky boilers, sprung plates and smashed stanchions. Holmans were often called out to the first two steam packets plying to the Isles of Scilly, the *Little Western* and the *Earl of Arran*. Long after they were wrecked on the islands, Holmans were busy repairing their successors, the celebrated *Lyonesse* and the *Lady of the Isles*, while the dry docking of the modern *Scillonian III* ensured the continuance of this tradition for 140 years.

Heavier marine work was done at Holmans' own foundry at St. Just, where the smiths became skilled in forging anchors, mast bands and iron beam knees for both fishing boats and the Penzance schooner fleet. Trinity House became an excellent customer from the early 1860s, ordering iron buoys, moor chains, and iron work for their beacons and lighthouses, from the foundry and, in later years, engine and machinery parts when the corporation entered the age of electricity and oil engines. The famous old Trinity House tender *Satellite* regularly had her boilers cleaned and engines overhauled by Holmans and they remained on the order books well into the 1980s, when many old manned lightships were converted to fully automatic at Penzance.

Although marine work became important to Holmans, they had no slip or repair yard at Penzance. There was a small dry dock, built in 1814 by the Matthews family of ship owners and merchants. This dock had been resited and enlarged when the harbour was rebuilt between 1880 and 1884, and given a new entrance in, what was later to become, the Abbey turning basin, while a swing bridge gave access from the sea. In 1894, the Mathews sold out their shipping interests, including the dry dock but, due to the untimely death of their father William, the Holman brothers were unable to make a bid. The dock passed to the Penzance Dry Dock and Coal Co., owned by a local ship owner, Sampson R. Taylor, who concentrated more upon importing coal than repairing ships.

A decade elapsed before the Holmans had another opportunity to acquire the dry dock and, once again, the death of the senior partner almost prevented a bid. John Holman died in May 1904 but was fortunately succeeded by Frederick Holman, a neat and dapper man, whose business and engineering talents were balanced by a lively interest in such disparate subjects as cooking, geology, gardening and the antiquities.

Frederick Holman oversaw the acquisition of the dry dock, which he and his brothers bought for £4,500 at an auction at the Western Hotel, Penzance, on 25th August 1904. They even considered shifting the main offices from St. Just, which must have made William Holman turn in his grave. He had always treated the Penzance branch as a 'sickly child', insisting that all orders

and decisions receive sanction from St. Just and requiring the nephew in charge to report weekly on the work in hand. The first vessel to be dry docked by Holmans was the Chester schooner *Margaret Murray*, which had been ashore off Porthleven.

There were frequent calls on the yard to repair vessels which had gone ashore on the Cornish coast. In September 1904, Frederick Holman drove to Lamorna, where the Scilly steamer *Lady of the Isles* lay beached and flooded in the cove. At the

The Scilly packet *Deerhound* dry docked in 1909, before she left Cornwall for Canadian waters.

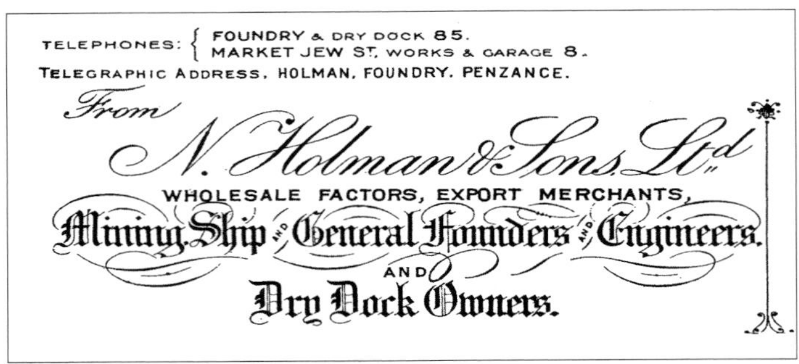

salvors request the shipyard hurriedly made bolt-on patches and the *Lady* was refloated, spending another thirty-seven years on the coast and becoming a regular customer for the dry dock. On another occasion, an encounter with the Land's End rocks in February 1906 put the collier *Stainburn* in the dry dock. Her repairs led to the famous incident when blacksmith Eli Gallie was held head downwards to rivet the inside of a tank!

Commercial work was interrupted by the First World War, when the dry dock was requisitioned by the Admiralty and came under naval control even to the extent of flying the white ensign above the offices. Holmans strove to oblige their old customers, such as Bennetts, Bain of Portreath and Harveys, but more often the dry dock was filled by a patrol trawler, minesweeper or fast anti-submarine launch. There were incidents galore. A live depth charge rolled off the deck of a trawler but failed to explode in the shallow water and was retrieved by a diver. An even bigger bang was avoided when a sea mine fell from crane slings and, bouncing off the bridgeworks, landed harmlessly beside a Holmans man and a naval engineer.

Several of the ships operating off Land's End were dry docked, in great secrecy, though everybody knew the hinged plates all over them were to hide guns. The crew of one of these 'mystery ships' tried to ensure their luck by catching and bringing onboard all the black cats they encountered. She swarmed with

The dock gates were made by Thames Ironworks but general repairs and maintenance on them were usually done by Holmans.

Holmans men with some of the crew on the bridge of the Newcastle steamer *James Spier*, which was bound from Liverpool to Bastia when she was rammed in dense fog by the Norwegian barque *Magdelen*, 30 miles SSW of the Scillies on 17 June 1903. Sailing ships usually suffered worst when arguing with steamers but the *James Spier* lost her mizzen mast and nearly sank, before the steam trawler *Buckhound*, of Hull, towed her in to be dry docked in Penzance.

Right: A regular visitor to the dry dock, throughout her career at Penzance, was the ex-Barrow schooner *William Ashburner*, operated by this date as a workhorse in the coal and cement trades, and owned by the Irish Kearon brothers. She is seen here standing on the keel blocks, displaying her classic lines although sadly reduced in rig, in 1934, not long after the completion of the new machine shops. Sailing ships were rare visitors to the dry dock, possibly only half a dozen in total being taken in by Holmans in the years since they took control. The *William Ashburner* hit a rock in the Severn near Beachley in about 1950. She was beached but drifted off and was lost for some time before grounding at Chepstow. There she was beached again and broken up where she lay.

The bows of the *Lady of the Isles* tucked into the corner opposite the dry dock offices of N. Holman & Sons. Holmans' St. Just foundry also made the ornate gas lamp standard on the right.

An unusual view, from a cracked negative, of *R.M.S. Scillonian* leaving the Abbey turning basin in 1934, having just come out of the dry dock following her winter overhaul.

them and a Holmans man, taking a fancy to '*a huge black Persian with a tail like a fox*', stuffed the animal down his shirt and sneaked ashore. The cat promptly took matters into its own claws; exploding with fury, it forced the thief to tear off his shirt and then bolted up the gangplank, back onboard.

In 1926, problems over the lease of the old wharf foundry convinced the directors to dispose of it and transfer the machine and founding shops to the dry dock. This was still occupied by a haphazard collection of leaseholders, including Joe Legg's boatyard and the Anglo American Oil Company depot. Several years elapsed before all the leases expired and Holmans could entirely clear the site but, by September 1933, the whole ramshackle layout had been replaced by a range of new machine shops, erected by John Lysaght & Co. Ltd. of Bristol. For some time they remained covered in brilliant red lead paint, much to the anger and consternation of the artistic community, before they were painted the now familiar dark green.

The dry dock was taken over again by the government at the outbreak of war in 1939 and the accumulated expertise with small ships meant that they docked many of the ubiquitous Dutch coasters serving under the Allied flag. To cope with the extra work new equipment, like electric welders, large lathes and a new dock pump, were installed; there were also the innovations of holidays with pay, trade union membership and female workers.

The immediate post war years found both the St. Just foundry and the dry dock in the doldrums. Another bid to move the head office to Penzance was again deferred and then came a disastrous venture when Holmans contracted to convert an old landing craft into a new ferry for the King Harry passage near Falmouth. This was closely followed by another serious setback when, in November 1952, the gates of the wet dock at Penzance, which Holmans had just refitted and rehung, were upset during a southerly gale. The heavy run of sea damaged several ships inside, including the coaster *Mount Blair*, which resulted in a 5 year legal battle between Holman's and the town council. To many it seemed that, after 120 years, Holmans were about to slip into oblivion but salvation came with a fresh and successful bid to reform both the management and direction of the Company. By early 1954 this was nearing completion, whilst the dry dock was being totally reorganised and overhauled.

After the reorganisation in 1954, the motor trawler *Excellent*, owned by W. Stevenson of Newlyn, was

The infamous steam collier *Treleigh*, owned by Bains and known to a generation of Portreath sailors as 'The Rolling Reggie', due to the sickening way she shoved her blunt bows into a head sea – crews would swear she even rolled in dock! Built at South Shields in 1894, she was a regular visitor to the drydock, as were all the Bain fleet, and was photographed undergoing repairs in about 1910.

The Workington collier *Stainburn* being dry docked stern first after being almost wrecked on the Runnelstone Rocks in February 1906. Assisting in the operation is the steam lighter *Jumbo*, owned by Captain James Chenalls of St. Just. Chenalls was a miner who became a ship salvor and subsequently worked all over the Bristol Channel. The *Stainburn* was lucky to reach port having caught fire following her encounter with the rocks, the flames only being doused by the water slowly flooding into her, as she passed Newlyn.

In June 1955, the arrival of the steam tanker *Pass of Melfort* heralded a new era for the Holman dry dock, which had fallen into the doldrums since the war. The yard was modernised to help cater for the refitting of the British coasting fleet and over 1,200 vessels were docked in the next 30 years. Holman fitters stand on the swing bridge to watch the tanker's arrival.

drydocked on Boxing Day of that year, the first of several such vessels and marking an upturn in Holmans fortunes. More important was the docking in June 1955 of the steam tanker *Pass of Melfort*, which marked the beginning of 30 years of service to the British Merchant Marine. She was followed by the coaster *Luminence*, one of the numerous 'Red Devils', owned by the London and Rochester Trading Company. The entire yard staff worked day and night to complete the job on time, finishing just as the water bubbled into the dry dock. In 1957, eleven ships were drydocked, the next year twenty one and the number increased yearly. The Company's archive contained a file on every ship docked since 1948, including coasters and tankers wearing the distinctive livery of F.T. Everard, or the grey-hulled tankers of the Esso Company, or the green painted ships of Metcalf Shipping.

In February 1963 Holman's launched the first ship at Penzance for almost a century, when they built the little steam tug *Primrose*, which saw fourteen years service. Another unusual job was the conversion of the tanker *Chartsman* into a floating tin recovery plant, to suck up tin bearing sand from the bottom of St. Ives Bay. In 1980, Holman's did their first conversion of a

Left top: The collier *Newport* manouevres gently into the dry dock, only a few years before she was wrecked near Portreath, whilst bound for Ilfracombe, during a north westerly gale on 27 January 1930.

Middle top: Over forty years seperate this view from the previous one but little has changed at the dry dock apart from the addition of a safety fence. The *Faience*, one of the 'Red Devils', the nickname for the London & Rochester Trading Company's fleet, is being dry docked after grounding on Hayle Bar in May 1971.

Middle bottom: Holman fitters pose for the camera whilst installing a new Kelvin engine onboard the coaster *Farringay*, in October 1966.

Left bottom: Escorted by the Penzance pilot boat *Vestal*, the coastal tanker *Shell Trader* puts to sea after a refit in the dry dock in September 1989, near the end of the Holman yard's years of working with vessels from the British mercantile fleet.

The *Fredrikstad* – before . . . .

. . . and after! Now a luxury motor yacht courtesy of the skills of the newly formed Penzance Dry Dock & Engineering Co. Note the sun glistening on the glossy paint finish of the hull.

manned light vessel to fully automatic, so successfully a dozen more followed her. The slow decline of the British Merchant fleet led the Company into more new pastures when, early in 1983, they docked the naval auxiliary *Yarmouth Navigator*. Like the *Pass of Melfort* 20 years before, it was the beginning of a remarkable chapter in the Company's history. The colours and flags of the coaster companies were replaced by the black and buff livery of the oilers, tugs, water and ammunition boats of the Royal Maritime Auxiliary Service.

Next to be seen was the camouflage of Army and Royal Marine landing craft; in May 1986, for the first time since submarine chasers were refitted in 1918, ships of the 'Old Grey Funnel Line' appeared in the dry dock, in the shape of the minesweepers *Carron* and *Waveney*. By 1992, two more of these handsome warships, the *Helford* and the *Arun*, had been successfully docked but the repercussions of the so-called 'peace dividend' were inescapable and Holmans once more tried to adapt to new circumstances. New contracts were sought from the old order books, such as ornate railings for a stately home, but it was not enough and the Company finally folded late in 1995.

The loss of the dry dock would have been a disaster for the town and the port but, thankfully, the long tradition of ship repairing at Penzance was rescued by Peter de Savory, the celebrated entrepreneur and yachtsman. By the spring of 1996, the Penzance Dry Dock & Engineering Company had taken over the shipyard and the flow of vessels for repairs and docking had resumed. Typical was the 80 tons of new steel work for the motor coaster *Sea Trent*. The star contract so far, was the conversion of the 75 foot ex-Norwegian rescue cruiser *Fredrickstad*, an ice breaker which had spent twenty years in Arctic waters and saved twenty five vessels. A sixteen month operation saw her totally stripped out and equipped as a motor yacht.

Despite its excellent reputation, the drying up of M.o.D. orders was too much for the yard to bear and after 91 years service, Holmans finally closed on 21 December 1995. The closure happened so quickly that the trawler *Conquest*, of Cairnbulg, was trapped in dock for some weeks, enabling the author to make his last dry dock drawing under the Holman banner. It was signed by all those still working in the yard at the time, including, top left, the Official Receiver!

Chapter 10
The Modern Port

'1st July. Wind SW, Force 4. Sea slight, Weather fair. Eddystone *from Sharpness, Cargo Cattle-cake. Captain Moyes. 'En route to Cobh: towed in engine trouble.'* Port Book, Penzance. 1977.

On a sunny afternoon in 1958, F.T. Everard's diesel coaster *Summity*, which was launched at Greenock only a few months before the outbreak of WW2, unloads bags of cement at the South Quay, onto a fleet of lorries belonging to Harveys of Hayle. A nostalgic scene, now lost forever, as the 1960s boom in road transport brought ever larger and faster lorries, and did away with the coasters completely.

Despite the loss of the outer harbour, most regrettably filled in to make a car park at the end of the 1950s, Penzance escaped the fate which radical changes in the nature of the coasting trade served out to other Cornish ports like Hayle and Portreath. Coal remained the biggest import, with thrice weekly cargoes being unloaded until around 1974 by a tracked crane, reputedly left behind by U.S. Army engineers after they embarked for D-Day. Thousands of tons of coal from Goole and Keadby, were shuttled from the quays along wharf road to the Gas works, whose tall brick retort house, filled with hissing and clanking machinery, dominated what is still called the Gas Quay, until it was finally demolished in 1972.

For a time after the war, into the early 1950s, scenes like this could still be glimpsed as an occasional horse and cart came out to meet the *Scillonian*, both at St. Mary's and Penzance.

J.H. Bennetts kept their own coal yard at the old Chyandour tin smelter, where they supplied their own business and other coal merchants, although only rarely were they asked to bunker some ancient steam coaster or trawler. Bennetts also had their long coal siding at Ponsandane, behind a row of 1930s railwaymens houses known locally as 'Little Moscow', but where the familiar 16-ton wagons were once unloaded there now stands a supermarket. Perhaps unique among Cornish ports, Penzance was for a time in the late 1970s an exporter of coal, if only dust and slack from the screening plant in the Chyandour yard, shipped to the continent in a variety of coasters. Among them was the ex Dutch coaster *Ekapn Chieftain* which, in September 1976, lifted the first cargo of 550 tons for Ghent, where it was processed into bricketts for export back to Britain.

The coal trade was, however, doomed, partly by the advent of road haulage but also by the disappearance of the traditional coal using industries, such as the mines and the gas works, by the gradual switch to central heating in the domestic market and to other, cleaner and more efficient fuels by industry. In July 1981 the author was still able to sketch sixteen coal lorries alongside the coaster *Gardience* but within a relatively short time coal ceased to be landed at Penzance. One of the last was delivered in August 1984 by the German motorship *Baltic Winter*, of hamburg. J.H. Bennetts concentrated on the booming bottled gas market, though retaining their shipping business and still proudly displaying their Lloyds Agency Plate outside their new offices on Causeway Head.

Many other regular cargoes had also gone or were going, stolen by juggernaut lorries or merely made redundant by changing demands. Coast Lines had stopped calling back in 1955, though their brass nameplate remained on the shed door for another twenty years and vanished just a day before the author decided to rescue it! The big concrete warehouse on the north quay was vacated by Ranks the millers in the fifties and had a variety of uses until taken over as a freight depot by the Isles of Scilly Steam Ship Company when they bought the *Gry Maritha*.

The beginning of the end! Late in 1959, the first lorry loads of quarry waste are tipped into the outer harbour, to provide a car park that would be a solution to the town's summer traffic problem. It was a crass decision, bereft of vision or economic sense, that would hamper future development in and around the port but it was the time when the motor car was in the ascendancy, and both water and rail transport lost out.

Coast Lines *Londonbrook* unloading coal at the West Quay for J.H. Bennetts in the early 1950s. The lorries and the crane all belong to the Penzance coal merchant; the latter was ex-U.S. Army, left over from the D-Day landings, and was always referred to as the 'Normandy crane'.

The old dock labour scheme went around the same time and with it a little known harbour tradition. In bad weather, when the *Scillonian* was delayed, the dockers retired to a clapboard shed where, to pass away the time, they indulged in their own version of 'sardines'; two teams sat back to back on a bench and bracing themselves, tried to heave their opponents onto the floor with such energy that, on one occasion, a large boot went through the side of the shed! Often too, mealtimes would be a time of further mayhem, when a 'pasty fight' could break out. A piece of pasty might accidentally fall on the floor but would then be picked up and casually lobbed at a workmate. In no time, meat and pastry would be flying round the shed, to the sound of shouts, hoots of derision and much laughter.

Cargoes of concentrate were regularly shipped out by Geevor Mine, the last being on the *Sant Antonicus* in 1987, a year after the mine was driven under by the tin crisis. Boxwood for the flower industry, until the advent of cardboard trays, was always a large cargo that often took a week or more to discharge from big foreign motorships like the magnificent *Arseny Mockvinn*, of Archangel, which called on voyage from the Black Sea in September 1976. An intermittent and quite amazing cargo are the enormous transformers which, bound for the electrical sub-station at Indian Queens in North Cornwall, are unloaded from ro-ro carriers like the *New Generation.*

Fishing did not equal the importance of the coal trade at Penzance until the arrival of beam trawling in the mid 1970s. The trawlers, equipped with a massive complex of wires, chains and derricks, found that welders, fitters and smiths were readily available alongside in the port. There was also the ill starred 'Mackerel Boom' which began in the winter of 1975 and soon saw the wet dock crowded with trawlers from Hull, Peterhead and as far away as Belfast and Barra. Many were large and powerful like the purse seiner *Gallic Rose* which, with water up to her combings, landed a record 115 tons of mackerel in January 1976. There were other much smaller boats like the *Sharon Rose*, of Buckie, on which the author recalls having an excellent dinner; the conversation, was held in a mixture of broad Scots and the equally strong accent of the author's home town of Camborne

During the late 1970s, the 'Mackerel Boom' saw Penzance as a base for a flotilla of trawlers large and small engaged in the bulk catching of the then vast mackerel shoals off the Cornish coast. Many came from Scottish ports like Buckie, Peterhead and even from Barra, in the Hebrides. The Peterhead boats pictured here are the *Faithfull II*, with *Stargazer* alongside and the *Accord* in front.

but the 'language of the sea' prevailed!

The boom also brought down a new generation of 'Yorkies', from Lowestoft, brand new stern trawlers like the *Boston Sea Harrier*, *Boston Sea Stallion*, *Boston Halifax* and the ill fated *Boston Sea Ranger*, which foundered off Gwennap Head during a southerly gale on 7 December 1977. There were also Dutch, Danish and Norwegian trawlers, as well as those from the Eastern Bloc, whose mother ships took on mackerel from any vessel that came alongside. Vast though the mackerel shoals were, they were decimated by this industrial fishing which caused deep resentment among the Cornish fishermen, especially the fleet of 'Toshers' whose crews, fishing with traditional handlines, saw a big netter scoop up what would provide their livelihood for months.

By 1982 the 'Mackerel Boom' was over and the juggernauts, ice shoots and fish elevators vanished from the quay sides. Penzance retains a small fleet of fishing vessels which use the wet dock to pain, repair or change their nets, though even their numbers are shrinking as the iniquitous 'Quota System' bites into the west Cornish fleets. Among those which range alongside are the *Scarlett Thread*, an ex-Scots boat which boasts a wheelhouse from a Danish trawler, the *Sowena*, a classic modern fishing vessel and the *Boy Antony*, an ex-Breton tunnyman whose fine lines owe much to the way they were copied from 'Mon peres' old ship (the captain's father's old vessel) and were duplicated in miniature when the author built a model of her in 1997.

Classic lines are not merely confined to wooden craft as the steel longliner *Dew Genen Ny*, Cornish for 'God with us' and launched at Aberdeen in 1975, has kept hers despite now having a shelter deck. The steel beamer *Girl Pat 111* is more impressive than pretty, with her funnel in the Cornish colours of yellow and black. The largest of the

A once familiar view now lost forever; looking towards the station with the part of the harbour that has been filled in on the right and the now demolished gas works on the left.

Several of the trawlers were lost during the time of the 'Mackerel Boom', including the *Conqueror*, a large freezer trawler from Hull, which was sheltering in Mount's Bay when she ran onto Penzer Point, at Mousehole, on 27 December 1977. Thankfully, the crew were all got off safely but it must have provided a moment of quiet satisfaction for Cornish fishermen whose own industry was being decimated by these huge 'factory' ships. The figure on the rocks is the author, unaware at the time that he was to spend the coming summer clad in a tattered wet suit salvaging gear and scrap from the wreck, which resembled Truro Cathedral lying on its side, half filled with water and rubbish. She was finally swallowed by an easterly hurricane on New Year's Eve 1978.

The purse seiner *Gallic May*, sister to the *Gallic Rose*, tied up alongside the West Quay around 1976. Behind her can be seen the little steam tug *Primrose*, built by Holmans in 1963 and nearing the end of her short life when this picture was taken.

regular callers is the steel beamer *Silver Harvester*, which was launched in Holland in 1968 as the *Jan Maarten* and served in the Brixham fleet, before coming to Penzance a decade later. She was soon lengthened by four metres amidships, which emphasised her elegant lines and she also boasts the longest derrick poles of any beamer in the bay. Resplendent in a livery of dark blue hull and white topsides, with a red and white banded funnel, she is unmistakable whether entering port or far out to sea.

The first major development of the harbour began when the century old Ross Bridge was replaced, by a modern steel swing bridge built by Visicks, of the Basset Works, Devoran, and opened by David Harris M.P. in 1981. Another antique mechanism fast approaching redundancy were the seventy year old wet dock gates; indeed, on New Years Eve 1981, the South gate sheered its pintles in a southerly gale and had to be lifted clear by the *Crazy Diamond*. Both gates still had to be opened by hand worked capstans, sailing ship fashion, a hazardous task in very rough weather, when they also had to be braced by heavy wooden booms. They were useless for a modern port and by the following spring the wet dock had been cleared of ships and sealed with a coffer dam, in an operation resembling the original harbour works of 1880. The new 'Flapdown' gate demonstrated its superiority over the old gates on the very day of the official opening, at 9.30 a.m. on 18 August 1982, lowering with ease despite a hard southerly gale, to admit the sludge tanker *Countess Weir,* led by the pilot boat *Vestal* and followed by the *Crazy Diamond*.

Throughout these years Penzance has always been a haven to an amazing flotilla of ships, some stranded by circumstance, others on a prolonged passage. In 1971, the harbour was home to both the beautiful steam yacht *Medea*, which ended her days as a preserved classic in California, and the big steel schooner yacht *Marea*, once the property of Grand Admiral Erich Raeder of the German Navy. The longest resident was the the ex-German coaster *Gloriosa*, which arrived in September 1980 and then lost both her captain and mate in a tragic accident onboard. Her new master, Captain Heinrich Westhuider, supervised the massive task of exchanging her main engine for that of the coaster *Eva V*. The latter eventually reached Penzance with her bows ballasted almost out of the water, as a few weeks before she had struck the Pierre Vertes, off Ushant. The mammoth job lasted well into the spring; in the meantime, the *Eva V*, having been sold for scrap, left under tow of the coaster *Caro* but, after various mishaps, was wrecked near Westward Ho! The *Gloriosa* finally sailed in July 1981 and the author still has fond memories of her and her Turkish crew, including the saga of rebuilding Captain Westhuider's bed, a seemingly simple task that was not finally accomplished until dawn.

The port of Penzance continues to thrive, even though times have changed quite drastically in recent years. Long gone are the days when coasters crowded the quays and today yachts and 'classic craft' outnumber the commercial vessels. The old Holman dry dock, which was more of an institution than a business, closed down in December 1995, although the Penzance

From the late 1970s through to the 1980s, cargoes of copper sulphide from Geevor, on the Penwith peninsula near St. Just, were regularly shipped from Penzance, the last going in 1987. These photographs show one of the first loads being delivered to the harbour by lorry from Geevor, **left,** in June 1978. It was tipped onto the West Quay and picked up by mechanical grab, to be loaded into the hold of the waiting ship, **right,** in this case the *M.V. Edelgard*, of Elesfieth in the old G.D.R. Copper sulphide is a residue of the tin ore processing and it was being shipped to Nonnskor, in Sweden, for smelting. **Top,** the *Edelgard* rides high in the water whilst waiting to be loaded .

Drydock & Engineering Company has resumed the work of refitting ships. Freight and passengers still crowd the quays when *R.M.S. Scillonian 111* and the *Gry Maritha* are in port, while the outer harbour, where the old mining schooners once moored up, is crowded with local yachts and pleasure craft. Maritime heritage has an increasingly inportant role and Penzance lies at the heart of a coastline whose maritime culture, history and traditions rival those of Brittany or the New England coast of America. The West Cornwall Maritime Festivals of 1996 and 1998 have charted the course for the way ahead and the historic port of Penzance looks forward to playing a still important role in bringing tourists and commerce to the town.

Left: In April 1977, the 190-ton grab dredger *Sandchime* became the first steam vessel to visit Penzance for many years when she steamed through the 'Gaps' and into the harbour. Launched by W. Simons of Renfrew in 1952, the old Admiralty pattern dredger had long been converted to oil fuel by the time she arrived here for scrapping. She was such a sturdy vessel that her demolition was postponed indefinitely and she was hired out to dredge the harbour. Captain Allan Riggall of Barrow Haven Marine bought her in autumn 1979 and replaced all the steam machinery, including the compound engine which went to a local industrial museum. Her characteristic funnel was removed in June 1981, since when the old dredger has worked as far away as Yarmouth and Southern Ireland.

Right: Another unusual visitor of the recent past was the Dutch cattle carrier *Jersey Express*, of Breskens. This dramatic photograph was taken as she came into port in May 1981 and records the near miss she had with a large tri-catamaran. The 'cat', under a single jib, chose to make a run for the harbour, wrongly assuming that the *Jersey Express* would give way, not realising that she was riding high and light in ballast, and was also being buffeted by an ESE gale.

Although the Scilly boats now comprise the main commercial traffic at the port, there is still the occasional cargo vessel calling. One very large load often landed at Penzance are the transformers bound for the National Grid electricity station at Indian Queens, some 40 miles up county near Newquay. They arrive on specialist heavy lift ro-ro ships like the *New Generation*, originally the *Kingsnorth Fisher*, seen here on the evening of 19 May 1996. She is disgorging a 298 ton transformer, mounted on a multi-wheeled trailer, which is raised to quay level by hydraulic ramps, the trailer then being towed off by a powerful Scammel tractor unit. The Scammel and trailer were provided by heavy haulage specialists A.L.E. of Stafford.

Chapter 11

The West Cornwall Maritime Festival and the Classic Ships

'The Festival at the Heart of the Celtic Seas'. Penwith District Council Promotional Slogan for 1998 Festival.

The handsome Dutch brigantine *Swan Fan Magnum* and the training brig *Royalist* quit Mount's Bay for Brest, in a stiff north breeze, after taking part in the highly successful West Cornwall Maritime Festival in July 1996.

The West Cornwall Maritime Festival has its roots in Penzance harbour's history as a coasting port and its geographic position. Although a surprising number of old time sailing coasters survived the war years, they were still so few that the sight of a ketch or schooner fast became a rarity in Cornish ports. One by one, vessels that for many years had been carefully entered in the port arrival books at Penzance were scrapped, wrecked or occasionally sold foreign, to the Baltic or Mediterranean.

In 1963, the iron schooner *Mary Stewart* called on voyage from Bude to Spain, commanded by Captain Peter Herbert who had given her hull a topcoat of green. It was mixed from every available spare can and she resembled the proverbial 'forty shades of green'. A decade before, Captain Herbert had worked the ancient Severn trow *Emperor* which, mastless and reduced to a motor barge, hauled scrap metal from the *Warspite* salvage operations. She was abandoned after being refused a load line and today her keel still lies embedded in the sand at Ponsandane.

As in the 1930s, the cement trade had continued to provide employment in the 1950s for various old windships, like the Barnstaple ketch *Progress*, which discharged phurnacite at Penzance in May 1950, before loading concrete blocks for Tresco. A regular visitor was the steel auxiliary *Result*, which ran numerous loads of coal, timber and cement to Scilly, and in May 1959 hauled a complete wooden chalet hotel to Tresco.

The *Result* would survive long enough to be preserved, though in the 1960s the concept of 'Classic Ships' was still far in the future. One ship that would have been well worthy of this title was the ex-Fleetwood pilot cutter *Falcon*, a pretty and elegant vessel, graced by the gilt figurehead of a falcon. After a refit at Penzance, she sailed for Gibralter in the autumn of 1963, only to be dismasted south west of Scilly and forced to put back. Many years later, she was sadly wrecked at Cawsand Bay near Plymouth.

Another regular visitor was the exquistly pretty brig *Maria Assumpta*, launched from the open beach at Badalona, near Barcelona, in 1858 and whose history is worth relating in full. She ran to Buenos Aires with general cargo on her maiden voyage and stayed in the South American trade for many years, hauling Argentinian beef, or shipping rum, molasses or tobacco for Spain from Cuban ports. By 1900, she was the *Pepita*, running in the salt trade from the Valencian port of Torrevieja to Morrocco, Brittany and Spanish ports. During the 1930s, she was fitted with a single cylinder oil engine and remarkably survived both the Spanish Civil and Second World Wars. Renamed *Cuidad de Inca* in 1946, she sailed out of the Majorcan port of Ibiza with her owner's other vessel, the elderly schooner *Veiguela*.

Like many old windships, the *Maria Assumpta* suffered the indignity of being reduced to a motored barge in her old age. By the 1960s, she had an ugly deckhouse and a funnel for the twin Baudoins which had replaced the ancient oil engine. Her rig was cut down to a stump foremast, which set a large trysail rigged on the derrick boom. She rarely ventured beyond the Mediterranean, hauling grain or salt and even cars or lorries were carried lashed athwartship, with their bumpers overhanging the bulwarks. By 1971, the *Maria Assumpta* had been reduced to a stores lighter for naval oil drums at Malaga and, once her engines had been sold, was destined to be burned at sea. She was saved for the cost of her engines by two enterprising Englishmen, who had her taken to Barbate, near Gibralter, where an Anglo-Spanish workforce virtually rebuilt her. After eighteen months, in June 1982, she was once more upon the oceans under full sail and in the following years voyaged around the Atlantic, to the Carribean and even up to the Great Lakes.

To celebrate her 130th birthday, she resumed sailing under the name *Maria Assumpta* and, by the 1990s, had become an increasingly popular and welcome visitor to Cornish ports. She was unmistakeable whether at sea or in harbour, quite literally a

Yachting has been enormously popular at Penzance since its earliest days as a resort. Here, the pretty yawl *Chocolate Girl*, a victor in the Regatta of August 1903, crusies before a breeze off the Promenade.

The small steam launch *Nora*, which used to do pleasure trips around Mount's Bay to Lamorna and the other coves before WWI. Her destination was indicated by the flag – in this instance Logan Rock and Penberth Cove.

A Century of Classic 'Little' Ships

The Thames sailing barge *Ethel*, disguised as the floating showroom *David Gestetner*, arrived at Penzance under the command of Captain Peter Herbert on 9 May 1976. Her sprit boom, a length of North Sea gas pipeline welded on a derrick, was found to be bent, so was removed by the Trinity House crane and repaired by a local blacksmith. The barge then spent three weeks in the harbour, windbound, before continuing her journey to Bristol. On her return in June, the author had the pleasure of sailing onboard around the Lizard to Falmouth. It was a hot summer day, with a fresh easterly wind and the sight of a Thames barge off the Cornish coast brought looks of amazement from passing ships. Captain Peter Herbert hails from Bideford and is one of the last of the old time Bristol Channel skippers. In the mid 1950s, he was the last man to take a sailing ship into Portreath, always a difficult harbour to enter, going in and out whilst a fellow skipper, in a motorised craft, stood off for three days waiting for the weather to improve.

A quiet afternoon in the 1970s, with the steam yacht *Medea* berthed under the concrete warehouse built for Ranks in 1935. Now over seventy years old, the *Medea* has ultimately found a home with a preservation trust in California.

Right: Now a true 'classic ship', the Tamar river barge *Shamrock* lies moored off Newlyn fishmarket in this 1962 photograph. Having finished a stint as a drilling boat, prospecting for tin in St. Ives Bay, she was working as a salvage ship around Mount's Bay and Land's End. According to waterfront legend, she was raising chunks of the boilers from the *Warspite* and, her diver having laid explosives, she motored to a safe distance. However, her crew were unaware that the line on which the charges had been lowered was still attached to their vessel. The detonation jumped the *Shamrock* out of the water and broke windows half a mile away onshore. Her colourful career might have ended on the mud of a Plymouth creek but, rescued and restored, she now resides at Cotehele Quay, on the Tamar, where she spent most of her working life.

A sight now lost to us forever following her tragic wreck in May 1995, the brig *Maria Assumpta* was photographed rounding up off the Lighthouse Pier in 1994. Then in her 136th year, she was the oldest square-rigger sailing upon the ocean seas, built originally of Spanish pine from the Forest of Montseny, behind Barcelona.

'pretty white bird of the oceans'. Her long career ended tragically in May 1995 when, inward bound for Padstow, she was wrecked on Pentire Head with the loss of three of her crew.

On a blustery and hot afternoon in June 1995, tops'ls to leeward of the Lizard heralded the arrival in Mount's Bay of the Russian barque *Kruzensthern*, one of the largest and most magnificent sailing vessels on the ocean seas. She hove to off Mount Mopus buoy, while the Lizard lifeboat and a Naval Sea King helicopter took off a sick crewman but the barque soon resumed her stately progress into the bay. By early evening, she was safely at anchor off the Promenade, swinging with the tide and a stiff NE breeze, her painted ports and soaring masts made bright by the westering sun. The *Kruzensthern* was only a year short of her seventieth birthday, having been launched at Westermunde in August 1926 as the *Padua*, the last of the famous 'Flying P' line of Hamburg. Like most of her fleet sisters, she was a typical latter day windjammer – a heavily rigged, four-masted, steel barque, built as a 'carrier' not a 'clipper', over 100 metres long and capable of lifting over 4,000 tons of cargo. She was handed over to the Russsians as war reparations in 1946.

The sight of such vessels in the Bay and the interest they caused was something to be considered. Then, in 1992, Penwith District Council Tourism Department was invited to the Brest Maritime Festival in order to promote West Cornwall as a tourist destination. Expecting a marquee and a few boats, they were amazed with what they were faced with – a huge event with hundreds of vessels, plus displays, stalls and presentations, with literally hundreds of thousands of people visiting and coming, like the boats, from all over the world. A seed was sown.

With its rich maritime history and situated midway between Ireland and the Brittany coast, Penzance was ideally located to hold such an event. A plan was prepared by the Tourism Department and presented to the Council, with backing being sought from the European Regional Development Fund, as well as private enterprise. It all resulted in the first West Cornwall Maritime Festival, held in July 1996 and adjudged a resounding success, attracting over one hundred boats and classic ships, and attended by in excess of 100,000 visitors. It put Penwith firmly back on the international tourist map once more.

The 1998 Festival will build on this triumph, with over a hundred and fifty boats expected, massive publicity across the country and round the world, and even larger crowds. The sight of classic vessels like the training ship *Malcolm Miller*, the brig *Royalist,* and the historic craft from 'Square Sail' at Charlestown, such as the newly refurbished *Phoenix* and the *Earl of Pembroke*, still proves an irrestible draw, as will be the anticipated visit of *H.M.S. Penzance*, a newly completed 'Sandown' class Minehunter and the first vessel to carry the town's name for over fifty years. Also attending are such craft as the French training ship *S.T.S. Jean de la Lune*, the French shrimper *Belle Etoile* and the Aubierne lifeboat, the *Tangeroa* and the environmental campaign vessel *Ocean Defender*. The town and harbour is being specially decorated for the event, including the completion of a series of murals, painted by the author, depicting the port's history.

Visiting once again just prior to the Festival is the great Russian barque *Sedov*, which came in 1996 at the invitation of the Tourism Department. She presented a truly magnificent sight but few of those who visited her realised what a remarkable vessel she is. She was launched in 1921 as the four-masted steel barque *Magdalen Vinnen* by the Germania shipyard at Kiel, part of the mighty Krupps armament and engineering empire. In keeping with most other German yards at the time, they were faced with the prospect of rebuilding the German merchant marine after

One of the largest and most magnificent sailing vessels still on the ocean seas, the Russian barque *Kruzensthern* is seen here at anchor in Mount's Bay in June 1995. She began life in 1926 as the German 'Flying P' line vessel *Padua*.

Reviving the days when devout Cornish Catholic pilgrims set sail from Penzance for Santiago de Compestella, the extraordinary replica of John Cabot's ship, the *Matthew* of Bristol, sails past St. Michaels' Mount outward bound from Penzance in July 1996.

The *Alexander von Humboldt*, an ex-German lightship built 1906, converted to a barque in the 1980s and now used by the German Sail Training Federation, in the harbour in November 1993.

The *Eye of the Wind,* a German iron schooner built in 1911 for the Rio Grande trade but more recently converted as a training brigantine, in the harbour in 1995. She was photographed moored alongside the distinctive white hull of the *Maria Assumpta*.

The French training schooner *Belle Espoir* lies at anchor off the South Pier awaiting the tide, whilst bound from Fowey to her home port of Brest in May 1979.

the First World War and had already launched the first of five big steel schooners for F.A. Vinnen of Bremen, who themselves were replacing vessels sunk or destroyed. The *Magdalen Vinnen* was to be the largest of their fleet, not a 'clipper' but, like the *Kruzensthern*, a 'carrier', capable of lifting 5,000 tons of Chilean nitrates or bagged grain from Spencer Gulf ports. Her spread of sail was enormous and, boasting wireless, electric light and auxiliary machinery, she was a well equipped as well as handsome vessel.

She was a good passage maker, though her auxiliary diesel engine, once destined for a U-boat, technically kept her out of the famous 'Grain Races' from the Australian ports. In January 1932, she was part of the remarkable fleet of latter day windjammers loading for the Channel in the Spencer Gulf; with her in Port Victoria were the barques *Lawhill*, *Melbourne* and *C.B. Pedersen*, and the big barquentine *Mozart*, while down the Gulf the 'Flying Ps' were loading and the beautiful *Herzogin Cecile* was in Port Augusta. The *Magdalen Vinnen* cleared for the Channel on 21 February and arrived off Gravesend ninety five days out, looking very smart and freshly painted, with her yards stripped. She moored close to the old training ship *Worcester*, whose cadets were given a tour of the great vessel.

Although manned by only a small crew of twenty eight and earning reasonable freights, the Vinnens decided she was no longer economic and, in 1936, sold her to the German mail line Nord Deutcher Lloyd. Renamed *Kommodore Johnson*, she became a 'Schuleschiff' and, shipping fifty officer cadets, returned to the grain trade, sailing over 100,000 miles by the time war came. She spent the war in the Baltic and, in 1946, like the *Kruzensthern*, was handed over to the Russians. In 1948 she was renamed *Sedov* and, after serving as an oceanographic research vessel, once again became a school, taking cadets wishing to join the Russian fishery fleets. Her visits to the Bay serve both as a fitting reminder of Penzance's maritime heritage, whilst at the same time adding a further page to it.

Building on the success
of '96 and '98, the intimate
Harbour of Penzance
looks forward to welcoming
you back to its third
MARITME FESTIVAL
in 2000
Cornwall's Premier
Tall Ship Experience

For information contact: 01736 362341

The Festival at the Heart of the Celtic Seas

The Russian barque SEDOV anchored off the Gear Pole rocks.

Patterns in the sails and the ship's bell – onboard the SEDOV.

Images of Classic Sail – The SEDOV – West Cornwall Maritime Festival 1996

Folding the sails neatly round the bowsprit – onboard the SEDOV.

Looking up the jigger mast of the square rigged barque SEDOV.